THE TAO OF BRUCE LEE

Davis Miller is the author of *The Tao of Muhammad Ali*. His writing has appeared in *Rolling Stone*, *Men's Journal*, *Esquire*, *Sport* magazine, *Sports Illustrated*, and numerous other periodicals. His first published story, 'My Dinner with Ali', was voted by the Sunday Magazine Editors Association to be the best essay published in a newspaper magazine in the US in 1989. It was a finalist for the 1990 National Magazine Award and in 1999 was judged by David Halberstam to be one of the fifty best pieces of sports writing of the twentieth century. His story 'The Zen of Muhammad Ali' was nominated for the 1994 Pulitzer Prize; that piece was later included in the 1994 edition of *The Best American Sports Writing*. Davis Miller has two children, Johanna and Isaac, and lives near Winston-Salem, North Carolina, where he was born. He is at work on several more books.

D1125383

BY DAVIS MILLER

The Tao of Muhammad Ali

Praise for *The Tao of Muhammad Ali*

'Nobody has ever written so purely about Ali before. Maybe no one has ever written so purely about anyone . . . An intimate, rambling, fascinating book . . . that is a low-key revelation, like a letter from an apostle.'

Los Angeles Times

'What Miller puts into perspective is the effect Ali has had on his, and so many other people's, lives. Poignant details are punctuated with metaphysical musings on existence. In essence, Miller is Ali's spiritual Boswell. A compelling, strange and beautiful book.'

Daily Telegraph

'Davis Miller has written a fine, rare book, one of only a very few that recognizes that sport can be a pathway to and for the spirit . . . *The Tao of Muhammad Ali* resonates with wisdom . . . A classic, part of the standard against which I'll measure all other sports writing.'

Glenn Stout, editor, *The Best American Sports Writing*

Davis Miller

THE TAO OF BRUCE LEE

VINTAGE

Published by Vintage 2000

5 7 9 10 8 6 4

Chapters of this book have appeared in different forms in
Men's Journal, the *Washington Post Magazine*, *Arena* (England),
Esquire (England), *M Quarterly* (Japan) and *Panorama* (Australia)

First published in Great Britain by
Vintage in 2000

Vintage
Random House, 20 Vauxhall Bridge Road,
London SW1V 2SA

Random House Australia (Pty) Limited
20 Alfred Street, Milsons Point, Sydney,
New South Wales 2061, Australia

Random House New Zealand Limited
18 Poland Road, Glenfield,
Auckland 10, New Zealand

Random House (Pty) Limited
Endulini, 5a Jubilee Road, Parktown 2193, South Africa

The Random House Group Limited Reg. No. 954009
www.randomhouse.co.uk

A CIP catalogue record for this book
is available from the British Library

ISBN 0 09 977951 X

Papers used by Random House are natural, recyclable
products made from wood grown in sustainable forests.
The manufacturing processes conform to the environmental
regulations of the country of origin.

Typeset by Deltatype Ltd, Birkenhead, Merseyside
Printed and bound in Great Britain by
Cox & Wyman Ltd, Reading, Berkshire

For Terry Davis

who has suffered through almost a quarter of a century
with this story and my writing

CONTENTS

ACKNOWLEDGEMENTS

Thanks first and foremost to Will Sulkin,
without whom I'd still be a lowly sports writer

To Doug Pepper,
the man with the US plan

To Gail S. Marion
for being the Doctor Baby
and for considerable patience through tough times

To Mel Berger
for not giving up this ghost

To Armand S. Deutsch
for being the greatest adopted grandfather of all time

To George Tan
who has lived this story more than I

To Peter Nelson
for the right *Curse of the Dragon* contracts

And to
Dennis Kennedy
Frank Lloyd Wright, Krishnamurti
Siddhartha Gautama, Bodhidharma, Alan Watts
Tom Simons

A ring centre bow to Professor Joe Lewis

For my martial mentors: Tony Lopez, Kathy Long, Li Siu Loong, Eric Nolan, John Chung

To Jesse Glover, and in memory of Ed Hart

To Dr Donald Langford

To Muhammad Ali and 'Sugar' Ray Leonard

To Laura Shepherd, Jan Wenner, Greg Williams, Bob Love, Kerry Shale, Glenn Stout, John Rasmus, Tobias Perse

---

To Jerry Douglas, Béla Fleck, Edgar Meyer and Russ Barenberg for organic and uncategorizable musical inspiration

To Harry Crews, Joan Didion, Nick Hornby, Tom Robbins and Tom Wolfe for being pointing fingers

To Holly Haverty-Woolson, for being my friend and for giving me one of the best lines I've ever stolen

And to everyone who has let me know how much my Ali stories have meant in their lives

AUTHOR'S NOTE

I'VE BEEN RIGOROUS in what I've written about Bruce Lee's life. I have not, however, allowed day-to-day details to get in the way of the larger truth of *my own story*.

A story must take on its own reality, a kind of story-reality. No story is accurate; many tell the truth.

Parts of this tale don't fit with other stories. Look at the edges of even the 'hardest', most immutable 'facts'. Look long enough, look honestly – the edges will shimmer.

Music's real. The rest is seeming.
Fats Waller

Dance as though no one is watching.
passed on by David Hebler

PART ONE

ENTER THE FOETUS

Show me a wonder
That you can't be sure of.

from a song by Walter Hyatt

ON MONDAY, 27 SEPTEMBER 1973 I was a drowsy-eyed, twenty-one-year-old freshman at Lees-McRae Junior College in Banner Elk, North Carolina. It was a miserable time in my life. I had few friends, inside or outside class. I lived vicariously through *Superman* comic books and the outsized deeds of Muhammad Ali.

I was five-foot-seven and weighed ninety pounds. Guys in my high school had nicknamed me 'Foetus'. I was punched in the stomach, pushed into girls' restrooms, had my skinny bones stuffed into lockers, or was plain ignored. Although most of my contemporaries were preparing to graduate from university and proceed into the real world, I was maturing slowly (if, and there was real doubt about this, I was growing up at all).

That September marked the first time I'd been away from my father's house for longer than a weekend. I was homesick. To relieve my misery, I spent time in Banner Elk's only cinema, drawn to the mystery and the power that lit-up screens and hidden speakers have when placed at the front of large, dark rooms.

Though Banner Elk's cinema was named the Center Theater, Lees-McRae kids called it the Bijou. Had it not been for them, the village of fewer than three hundred residents could not have supported a cinema. Directly behind my dorm and at the end of the car park, the Bijou was about the size of, and maybe half as clean as, a greasy old two-car garage. Tickets cost twenty-five cents each. A different feature opened every three days. Since the beginning of term, I'd seen almost every film that was shown at the Bijou.

The picture that night was *Enter the Dragon*. The house lights dimmed, flickered, went out. The red Warner Brothers logo flashed.

And there he stood.

There was a silence around him. The air crackled as the camera moved towards him and he grew in the centre of the screen, luminous.

This man. My man. The Dragon.

One minute into the movie, Bruce Lee threw his first punch. With it, a power came roiling up from Lee's belly, affecting itself in blistering waves not only upon his onscreen opponent, but on the cinema audience.

A wind blew through me. My hands shook; I quivered electrically from head to toe. And then Bruce Lee launched the first *real* kick I had ever seen. My jaw fell open like the business end of a refuse lorry. This man could fly. Not like Superman – better – his hands and his feet flew whistling through sky. Yes, better: this wasn't simply a movie, a shadow-box fantasy; there was a seed of reality in Lee's every movement. Yet the experience of watching him felt just like a dream.

Bruce Lee was unlike anyone I (or any of us) had seen.

'It is not the vulgarity of James Arness pistol-whipping a drunken, stubbled stage robber,' legendary folksinger Phil Ochs wrote of the first time he saw Bruce Lee:

> It is not the ingenious devices of James Bond coming to the rescue, nor the ham-fisted John Wayne slugging it out in the saloon over crumbling tables and paper-thin imitation glass. It is the science of the body taken to its highest form, and the violence, no matter how outrageous, is always strangely purifying.

In *Enter the Dragon* Bruce Lee moved fluidly, almost Alisweetblack, but with a rhythm distinctly his own. And, *oh!*, was he fast. Even faster than Ali. So explosively quick that the paths of his hand strikes were invisible. You could see techniques begin and end – nothing in the middle. It hardly seemed possible. Yet here he was, right in front of me, right here on this shimmering twenty-foot-tall screen.

Fists flying, feet soaring, punching and kicking bad guys from all angles. Punches and kicks – and much, much more. Lee's limbs moved in such a marvellously precise fashion that, when he was facing the camera, his blows seemed to slice the screen into sections. In addition he was the only genuinely lithe man I had ever seen, other than Ali. (Women are sometimes lithe, I believed; men almost never.) Lee used hands and feet, knees and elbows, shoulders and head, *good great God, his entire body*! And he did so with just about perfect grace and balance.

Even more amazing: when he was standing still, something inside him vibrated; something continued to move.

Another big part of his appeal for me was that Lee was only about my size. Though he seemed invulnerable, he was short and thin and there was a fragility, an eggshell mortality, about him. If this little guy could be this righteous, whuppin' huge bad guys with such unthinkable speed, power, accuracy and ratifying beauty, I could, too.

I was off to the moon.

Oh, hell, no! Not the moon. Neil Armstrong had already made that voyage. I was up, up and away, on the first manned mission to Alpha Centauri.

Bruce Lee was a master of effortless effort, an artist whose brush strokes sliced the air, and opponents' bodies, as naturally and unerringly as ancient Buddhist

5

monks had spent only seconds stroking watercolours into bamboo patterns on rice paper, patterns signifying Five Virtues of the Superior Man – simplicity, harmony, wisdom, contentment, a life beyond ambition.

Ali had seemed so singular, so freaky, such a mutant. And he was so damned huge. Bruce Lee's frame, the length of his arms and legs, the ratio of upper body to lower, looked almost exactly the same as my own, though I didn't consciously think about any of that.

What I knew in every molecule in my body was this: Bruce Lee was who I'd always wanted to be, what I'd always believed I could become (or, more precisely, *felt* I was already in some unseen way), although, before meeting Lee, I wasn't certain such a person could exist.

2

THE END OF summer of my eleventh year. As usual, I walk through the living room to the den. Though the sun hasn't cleared the tops of oaks and sycamores behind the house, aunts and uncles and grown-up cousins are sitting on our new sofa and chairs and are standing on the back porch smoking cigarettes.

My Aunt Anna and my father's Aunt Johnnie guide Carol and me to the kitchen table and bring us each a plate with a powdery white doughnut on it and a glass of watery orange juice which makes my stomach hurt. When we've eaten, Carol and I are led to our parents' room, where Daddy is seated on the bed. He pats the mattress on either side of him, asking us to sit. Someone closes the door.

Daddy draws a deep breath. 'God must've needed a blonde-haired, blue-eyed angel,' he says, calm and level.

Carol leans forward, looking at me across Daddy's lap. 'What does that mean?' she asks, her eyes sleepy, her mouth open, her voice soft and trusting.

'It means . . .' I hesitate; I'm not sure what it means. Then: 'It means Mommy's dead,' I say.

As the words leave my mouth, I know that they are true. A swarm of hornets rises in my chest and flies through me. My face stings, my hands do, too; so do my eyes.

I run from the room, down the hall, into the kitchen. I stare out of the alcove windows at cars passing on the

7

street. How can everything look the same when all of it has changed for ever?

'I'll kill them, I'll kill them all,' I say, not knowing who I'm talking about, then knowing that, too. 'I'll kill every doctor I ever see,' I say.

And Aunt Anna comes and pulls me to her breasts and rocks me slow and gentle. 'I'll kill every doctor in the world,' I say through clenched teeth, not feeling my Aunt Anna at all.

And Daddy closes and locks the door to the room he's shared with my mother. And he begins to wail and howl from somewhere so deep inside I could not have guessed such a place existed.

My mother, Sara Burns Miller, had died, aged thirty-two, of a kidney disease we did not know she'd had, although she'd been sick all my life. I've always believed that my mother's death is the most significant thing anyone could learn about me. And I also believe that it helps explain a great deal about how Ali and then Bruce Lee came to be so important in my life.

My mother. Much of what I know about her can be found in the hundreds of photographs she took of me. These pictures share many qualities. I'm always dressed in doll-like perfect clothing. I'm almost always alone, standing glowing and perfectly formed in near-perfect light. I'm wearing a perfect camera-gobbling smile and have JFK perfect hair: visible manifestations of my mother's compulsive ache for everything to be understood, in control and, well, perfect (her health never was), an anxiety she passed on to me.

Within days of her death, I quit blaming doctors and placed the fault where it really belonged – on me. Mommy's doctor had advised her not to have children. But she had had me and then my sister. I thought Carol and I had made her die.

With this recognition, I shut myself away from every-one around me. When Daddy tried to talk with me, to pull me from my impermeable funk by asking questions, I answered not in words, but with grunts. By late Novem-ber, when John Kennedy was killed, my catatonic forcefield was fully charged. By the spring of 1964 I'd not only quit talking, I'd just about stopped eating (during meals my stomach cramped so bad I'd fall to the floor, roll up in a ball, and rock back and forth in moaning pain), I'd quit playing with Carol and with other kids, and I came out of my shell only to watch Ali on Daddy's tiny black-and-white TV, to play by myself in the woods and down at the creek behind Daddy's house, to go to and from school (where I'd stopped doing work and sat staring at initials carved in my desktop, wondering when I'd wake from this awful dream), to buy comics and Tom Swift books, and to go to the movies.

The Carolina Theater was the last of Winston-Salem's stately old movie palaces. Inside it was adorned with ornate silver sconces; marble statues of gods, goddesses and heroes; a wide, winding, red-carpeted staircase designed to make each of us, one and all, feel born of royalty; and a must-laden, stiff, faded and stained once-red velvet curtain that looked as if it weighed about a hundred tons.

On Saturday mornings at nine o'clock the dust-heavy curtain rose and, after paying ten cents admission, children twelve and under were shown a cartoon and a weekly episode of a Radar Man, Batman or Superman serial; we played bingo for movie passes, popcorn, sodas and candy; and we watched a full-length cowboy or monster picture.

On Friday and Saturday nights Daddy would take Carol and me to a Western or to a Disney. I remember a summer evening in 1964 when Carol was spending the night with a friend. I recall riding in the car with Daddy and that the windows were down. Crickets and cicadas were throbbing; it was one of those nights so steamy and still that it seemed to float up against your skin. I remember stopping for a cone of soft-serve vanilla ice cream on the way to a double-feature at the Winston-Salem Drive-In. And, as the sticky ice cream dripped across my fingers, Daddy said, 'Need to tell you 'bout these movies, son.' His words, his tone and the look on his face were obviously intended to carry weight.

'You'll see some things with women you never seen,' he continued. I didn't understand what he meant, only that he sounded nervous, protective and maybe a little guilty. 'Nothin' to get worked up about, Dave,' he assured me.

The movies that night were *Doctor No* and *Goldfinger*. Hours later, *entirely* worked up, I lay wide awake in bed, hearing the movie voices inside me, recalling not women on the screen, but how James Bond had been so screw-everybody-cool, and how he'd disposed of all bad guys, effortlessly and systematically, the power magically vested in him by late-twentieth-century technology and by a strange, mystical Japanese science called 'karate'.

A few weeks later, Daddy told me about a new TV show, *The Man from U.N.C.L.E.* We watched the first episode together. And here they were again, these secret agent types, these coolest of the cool. To me, the hero, Napoleon Solo, was badder than Bond, cooler than zero, as he hiply and virtuously battled, and almost effortlessly destroyed, each and every foe. He was seldom, if ever, hurt in return, having been rendered indestructible (and nonchalantly cocky!) by near-magical gadgetry, and by knowledge of that same exotic and miraculous 'karate'.

Over the next four years I ached to become Agent Solo. On weekday afternoons, until it was time for Daddy to get home from work, I crept from room to room in the house, shooting evil counter-agents (who fell bloodlessly dead before my eyes) and delivering lethal karate chops a

10

hair's breadth away from lamps, bedposts, the hat rack beside the front door and (my favourite place of all) the back of the neck of the skinny, long-legged, trembling, six-pound female terrier my mother had bought and named Black Jet.

As five o'clock approached, I began to pace back and forth from Daddy's bedroom window to the kitchen alcove, watching for his car to come around the bend in the road. 'Dear God,' I'd plead to the walls and windows, 'please let Daddy come home NOW.'

In winter months it would be dark before I'd see the left-turn indicator winking on Daddy's Impala. As the sun set, I'd get big anxious and large agitated. I'd race from bedroom to kitchen, kitchen to bedroom. As I ran from one end of the house to the other, when Carol got in the way, Jet wasn't the only one who suffered showers of karate chops.

On weekends I asked Daddy to drive me from pharmacy to toy store to department store, where I collected *The Man from U.N.C.L.E.* accoutrements – trading cards, magazines, books, guns, badges, walkie-talkies, stereo LP records.

The Man from U.N.C.L.E. was last shown on NBC on 15 January 1968, my sixteenth birthday. To me, its passing was a major event. The year before, for refusing to be inducted into the army, Ali had been stripped of his licence to box; surely he was on his way to jail. I had no friends by then, only Napoleon Solo books, some pulpy boxing magazines and the now darkened television.

All through my teenage years, each weekday morning, after Daddy'd fixed a hot breakfast for Carol and me and placed it on the table, he'd playfully march from the kitchen, down the hall and into my room to wake me. All the way down the hall, he'd optimistically, rousingly, cheerfully sing. 'Daaveee, Davy Crockett, King of the

11

Wild Frontier,' he'd serenade, cartoonishly exaggerating every syllable.

And 'I can't get 'em up, I can't get 'em up, can't get 'em up in the morning. I can't get 'em up, I can't get 'em up, can't get 'em up at all.' It may have been the only military song he knew. Daddy came of recruiting age after World War Two. By the time American soldiers were fighting in Korea, he and my mother were married, I'd been born, and he was exempt from service. Thank goodness.

Daddy was such a wondrously gentle man, I believe that military training would've ruined him, put him in a state where he would've had greater difficulty honouring/allowing his compassionate and tender nature. (Growing up stoically during the Depression and World War Two in the industrial South, the son of alcoholic parents, and losing his only childhood sweetheart when they were both so very young, I still marvel at his uncommon tenderness.)

On weekday mornings, when Daddy tried to wake me, I couldn't open my eyes, couldn't force them open, not after ten, fifteen, twenty minutes, sometimes even half an hour. 'Son, come on now,' he'd say, trying to sound only a little irritated, 'I'm gonna be late to work. Get on up and go to the bathroom and splash some cold water on your face.'

Many mornings, he'd take me by the hands, tug me from bed, lead me to the bathroom, turn on the water, splash it on to my face. No matter how hard I tried (and I did), I still couldn't open my eyes.

3

MONDAY EVENING, 27 SEPTEMBER 1973. I watched – and heard and *felt* – Bruce Lee smack hundreds of people so hard and fast that they froze where they stood, their neuro-circuitry scrambled. They bowed, they fell, they lay. And they didn't get up.

To me, this was high art and science; each moment, every movement, was rivetingly righteous, sanctifying, purifying – a steaming hot bath on a frozen night.

At the end of the last luxurious battle in *Enter the Dragon*, I looked at the world around me for the first time since Lee had appeared onscreen. Compared to the song his body had sung, my existence was cold, mechanical, tedious. A moan, a Holden Caulfield whine.

I had no illusions about *Enter the Dragon* being a great film, or even a good one. It was more of the same Bondish junk I'd seen a thousand times and outgrown years before. *Enter* itself hadn't so affected me; it was Bruce Lee, who'd leapt, shining, from the screen.

As I left the cinema, I didn't walk; I glided about a yard off the ground. As soon as I'd seen Lee, in that single incandescent moment, I knew: I had not even known what martial art was. Now an extraordinary new reality had been revealed. And that reality purred, for me, in a way nothing else had. What I had believed, abstractly, about who a martial artist could be had been defined, precisely, by Bruce Lee, this man who single-fistedly manifested so many of my ideals.

13

When I'd stumbled upon Lee in *Enter the Dragon*, I was a prospective monk finding an ancient Taoist scroll in the bargain bin at a small-town five and dime.

Enter left town on Thursday. But I needed more time with Lee. Friday, instead of driving to Daddy's house, which I'd done every weekend since I'd started college, I tooled over to Johnson City, Tennessee, where the movie'd been showing for a month and a half. At the door, a beautiful, dark-featured girl gave me a smile and a copy of a magazine called *Fighting Stars*, which featured Lee on the cover. It was one of only a couple times in my whole life that a good-looking girl had smiled at me.

What did it matter that she handed copies to people in front of me and behind? Those people were spectators, who floated from one sideshow to the next, seldom understanding – or curious to understand – what performance(s) they were seeing; wanting a performer, any performer, every performer (whether Lassie, Elvis, Sinatra or Jesus), to deliver them, for a time, from boredom. I believed I was different. This was the reason the beautiful girl had shared her smile with me.

Bruce Lee was a participant, a mover; I wanted to become one, too. And *Fighting Stars* would be the second chapter of my mystagogy; it would help introduce me to knowledge that might prove to be the peer of my well-worked martial pretensions.

4

I DIDN'T KNOW until I got to my dorm room, opened the magazine and read the hurriedly written obituary on page one – Bruce Lee was dead at the age of thirty-two.

I almost had to sit down on the floor. I couldn't see how or why someone so obviously alive could ever really die, at least at the age Lee had.

Thirty-two, the same age Ali would be on his next birthday. And one year younger than Jesus had been when he went out and got himself offed. Most important to me, though, it was the same age my mother was when she'd died ten years before.

Christ, I wouldn't even have thought Lee was thirty-two. He looked mid-twenties, tops. A man so youthful, how could he be dead? Especially when he was the guy I'd hoped to find for so many years – and had only just met.

At sixteen I was four-foot-ten, weighed sixty-three pounds, and felt powerless and forlorn almost all the time. It's an understatement to say that I had no interest in school. I flunked nearly every class on my schedule, I had failed the tenth grade (and would eventually fail the eleventh) and when Daddy tried to talk with me about doing something with my life, pleaded with me to get interested in anything, I told him that I already knew what I wanted and what I was qualified for – and I didn't need good grades to make it to the welfare rolls.

15

For my birthday present, hoping to capture The Power that Ali and Bond and Superman tapped into, I asked Daddy for karate lessons. The instructor we chose didn't look like Bond, Ali or Superman; he was short, Italian, overweight, and by day worked as a hairdresser.

Daddy drove me to every karate class and I worked as hard as a sixty-three-pound runt could – punching and kicking the air in front of other skinny kids for an hour and a half three nights a week; sweating and hurting under fluorescent lights that made my skin look splotched and blue.

Workouts stimulated my appetite and my confidence. I dressed spiffy and made friends. 'Kid Karate', girls wrote in my junior yearbook. The year before no one had signed my annual; the few guys who'd talked to me had called me 'Pissant' and 'Foetus'.

During karate class, the big, round hairdresser/instructor told us of great spiritual powers he possessed, and about little Japanese gents who catch arrows in midflight, break concrete blocks with their heads, punch through watermelons, chew and swallow glass, kill with a single, seemingly ordinary, touch. Whenever *Sensei* was asked to demonstrate his skills, he gracefully declined, explaining that The Secrets were too powerful to show to just anyone.

So. I kept sweating and hurting and kicking and punching and sweating under the lights, hoping to become good enough to learn The Secrets.

And *Sensei* kept telling his stories. The one about the old, shrivelled and blind Buddhist monk who lived near Kyoto, and who had fought in, and been the survivor of, over 1,500 one-on-one death matches. And the one about Count Nakamura, who'd been blessed with the gift of the Iron Palm by one of the ancients. No one could survive one of Count Nakamura's Iron Palm strikes. And of the many immortal, invincible Japanese masters, whose eyes radiated a strange white heat and upon whom no one dare look.

I believed the stories. I needed to.

After a year and a half of blistering work, practising stances and forms, flicking hand strikes and kicks at mirrors in class and for an hour alone in my bedroom every night, I earned a brown belt, the rank immediately below black. In the interim, I'd grown to be a five-foot, eighty-pound stud, after finally reaching puberty. I'd soon learn one of The Secrets.

Not from my hairdresser/karate *Sensei*, but from Alvin Lindsor.

Alvin was the second smallest kid at school. He weighed eighty-eight pounds and was two years younger than me, though we were in the same grade. He was a standout member of the varsity wrestling squad, fought with the Gladiators Amateur Boxing Team, stole beer from 7-Elevens, and whupped up on bigger kids in his spare time. No one dared call Alvin by anything but his name.

The high school Alvin and I attended, Mount Tabor, was housed in a brand-new one-storey brick building, the institutional equivalent of 1960s ranch-style houses. Mount Tabor was the Winston-Salem/Forsyth County School Board's experiment in progressive education. Basic English, maths and health classes were taught by television sets. Sports history was offered as an alternative to senior English. Troublemakers weren't kept after school in teachers' offices or classrooms. Minor offenders – those rampant hormone cases who'd been caught chucking spit wads at Mr Evans, the gay biology teacher, chomping gum in Mr Morris's English lit class, arriving tardy for Miss Ooten's home-room, or hunkering over fifteen-year-old Julia 'Jugs' Jordan's rather obvious physical virtue(s) – would report to Detention Study Hall promptly at three-fifteen, where they'd spend the next sixty minutes. Detention Study Hall was housed in the cafeteria. Alvin and I were charter members.

DSH, as we habituals called it, was founded on the hopeful assumption that if strays were herded into a central keeping pen where they'd be overseen by a single trail boss, cattlehands would be free to complete their chores unhampered. I first suspected the Secret in DSH. It was a Monday afternoon in February 1971 and I was serving a sentence for refusing to change for phys. ed. (I didn't dare undress in front of anybody, anywhere, even if a teacher said I had to and even if all the people around me were just guys.)

I was sleeping at the far end of a yellow Formica-topped table and, when I woke and looked up, Alvin, who'd been sitting near the opposite end when I'd gone to sleep, was standing over me, holding my history book open in front of my face. Spit was rolling from its pages.

He closed the book, laid it on the table, walked to his seat, slapped hands with a couple wrestler buddies and sat down beside Sam Stone. Stone was short and bunchy muscled and had the same burning steel-grey eyes I envisioned the great karate masters having. Stone was twenty-one years old and was in the eleventh grade. My sophomore year, when sitting beside him in DSH, he'd ripped a sleeve from my sweater and cut a quarter-inch-deep hole in my back with his pocket knife, all for fun. It was stuff like that, and the magma in his eyes, that made everybody think Stone was a genuine maniac.

Out of the corner of my eye I saw Stone pass Alvin something, maybe a note, under the table. Alvin glanced down at it, then rose from his seat and ambled over. I began to sweat. Stone was looking past Alvin and at me. There was a glint in his eyes.

Alvin glared down hard at me, then lowered his right hand to my bony excuse for a left biceps, which he squeezed a little, before sliding it across the shoulder of my crisply starched, almost brand-new 'Beau Brummel' shirt (the more starch, the stiffer the exoskeleton, the more substantial the man), and up to the collar, which he wrenched into a knot. I reached to straighten it. Alvin slapped down my hand.

'Hey, you, you fuckin' Foetus, you. You got a lotta people fooled, actin' like you got some karate corncob stuck up your ass. But me and Stone, we know what a pussy you are.' He thrust a jaggedly bitten fingernail a couple inches from my nose. 'Tomorrow, I'm gonna make you eat shit off that corncob, turdface.'

Mr Hayes, the gym teacher who'd made me stay after school, was in charge of DSH that week. He didn't look up from the magazine he was reading. Alvin's friends laughed. Long, high, cackling laughter that made my arms and legs feel frozen stiff to the ground.

I skipped first period the next morning. When I walked into home-room everyone was talking about the inevitable 'War of the Midgets'. At Mount Tabor, Miller–Lindsor would be as much the Fight of the Century as the Muhammad Ali–Joe Frazier bout that would take place in less than two weeks.

Most students and a few teachers were placing bets on who'd win. Rumour had it that Mr Cole, the wrestling coach, had twenty dollars on Alvin. Supposedly so did the principal, Mr Hearty, who'd been a Golden Gloves boxer. Fourteen-year-old Batman, Green Hornet and James Bond fans were betting their quarters on me.

To get out of second period study hall, I volunteered to deliver mimeographed copies of the list of absentees to teachers. Alvin and my sister were in the same Spanish class. Carol was sitting close to the front of the room. Along with the other hardasses, Alvin was near the back, using his hands to play the drum solo from *Wipe Out* on his desktop.

Miss Rapley, the Spanish teacher, was the only black woman who taught at Mount Tabor. And she was my favourite person in the whole school. I had Spanish with Miss Rapley fourth period, before lunch. Every Friday she played Santana records in class and told us stories about her college internship in Argentina. She'd wander from desk to desk, singing songs in that beautiful language which made her better than us. One Monday a couple weeks before the end of the year Miss Rapley suddenly wasn't in class and Mr Hearty was, telling us she wouldn't be back. She'd been busted for her night-time and weekend business – selling marijuana out of her little garage apartment across from campus. After Mr Hearty introduced us to our new teacher, I walked out of class and never went back.

This February morning, though, when I passed Alvin on the way up to Miss Rapley's desk, some guy I didn't know, sitting next to Carol, yelled, 'There's that Karate Kid Miller that Alvin's gonna beat crap out of.'

'Alvin couldn't whup me with a baseball bat,' I said almost instantly, not only in defence of my pride and my family's, but in defence of the Japanese martial arts.

Guys laughed and made oohing sounds and somebody behind Alvin pushed his shoulders, prodding him on. Miss Rapley slipped an arm around my shoulders and escorted me from the room, gently closing the door behind me.

'Here, catch,' shouts the man. He's standing several yards away. I'm not wearing my glasses; I can't see his face. A long wooden object tumbles toward me a couple feet over my head. I try to grab it. My timing isn't good. The wind sings through it as it passes by my hands; it makes a plopping sound as it drops into the perfect middle of a pool of water behind me. I don't realize until I turn and see Silas Creek that I'm standing near the end of Daddy's

backyard. The object floats downstream. I reach into trousers' pockets, find my glasses, put them on.

The man has disappeared. The object is a bamboo flute. I want that instrument. I feel the need to learn to play.

I stand on the bank, scared to jump into the stream. Even though I know the water will feel ssooo fine, I'm scared of what may lie beneath the surface – jagged thrusting rocks, giant jutting shards of glass, knife-finned carp, alligator snapping turtles, sea snakes, dragons, Ninjas, mud, Joe Frazier, my mother.

And I'm scared because I don't know how to swim. But the water in the creek is never deeper than waist height, even after the worst summer storms. I follow the flute as it floats downstream, tumbling over and around rounded stones, making musical bumping sounds. The current isn't fast; there's no need to run. It's easy to walk along the bank and stay parallel to the rolling bamboo reed.

But why do I find it so hard to jump in? Particularly if I want the flute so bad.

I didn't go to school the next two days. Usually, when I skipped class, I stayed in the building, creeping down the halls from one bathroom to the next, combing my hair and throwing hand strikes at my reflection in the mirrors above the sinks.

This time was different. I could say I had a purpose. I pretended to be sick until Daddy left the house, then I got out of bed and worked out hard both days – and both nights in *Sensei*'s class – making myself look forward to the grand opportunity that Alvin had given me to showcase my rarefied skills.

Tiger Claws, Dragon Rakes, Dream Fists. Prisms of light leap effortlessly from my fingertips. Alvin falls before me and is grateful to have received a lesson in the fistic mysteries from his obvious superior.

Friday morning, I dressed in the pants to my green pinstripe suit and took extra time combing my hair so I'd look pretty for the fight. Daddy drove Carol and me to school. He let us out at the entrance and Carol went ahead of me. As I opened the door to the building, an 'honour guard' of wrestlers and football players appeared from wherever they'd been waiting. They escorted me to Alvin, who was standing with a large pack of friends around the corner.

I cocked my head to the side and put on my very best swagger for him. He sneered at me. 'Good mornin', faggot,' he spat. 'How come you never go out with no wimmin? You like men better, don't you, faggot?'

Before I had a chance to say anything, he slapped me, hard, on the right cheek. My glasses flew from my face and ricocheted with a hollow metal sound off the row of lockers behind me.

I felt The Secret then, first in my stomach, next in my throat, but I pretended it wasn't there and shoved it back in my belly. 'Hey, man, not in here,' came a voice from somewhere. 'Take him to the parking lot.'

Someone passed me my glasses. I put them on; they were lopsided. I remember floating out the door and across the asphalt, feeling the crowd grow around us. Alvin led me to the end of the lot and up a short grassy hill, where we stopped in front of a stand of yellowed scrub pines. I glanced behind me at the sea of people. All two thousand Mount Tabor students, *and their parents!*, had to be. I handed my glasses to a stranger. Jesus, what a bunch of faces. 'Break his ribs, Alvin.' Faces, full with a mean kind of joy.

I lowered myself into the deep, strong, bent-legged horse stance I'd practised for what seemed endless hours in karate class (legs so far spread it looked as if I was trying to straddle the Pacific Ocean), and chambered both fists in the inverted *hachiji-dachi* position on the waist, elbows flat against the sides, chest thrust out, neck high and rigid, exactly the way *Sensei* had taught.

Alvin stared at me incredulously, until he realized I intended to fight from that stance. Then his eyes relaxed. 'You gonna try'n kick me, pussy?' he said, smiling, and he tucked his chin in next to his shoulder and raised both fists to ear level. 'Only girls and faggots kick each other,' he said, laughing.

He took two steps to the left and I turned with him, determined to face him no matter where he moved. He pushed an open palm into my nose, pulled it back. I kept both fists at my sides. He slapped me across the mouth, and again. I tried to deflect the second blow with the rising, looping, outside, *age-uke* block I'd been taught in class. It was too stiff and too slow. Alvin jabbed me, close-fisted, and hooked off it. The punches didn't hurt, only numbed my face. I kept both fists chambered at the waist. Alvin slid two more jabs into my chin; my head twice slammed the back of my shoulders. He laughed once more. Much of the crowd laughed with him. Their laughter thundered over me. Soon I was lost in the thunder.

Alvin tackled me at the waist, I fell jarringly on to my shoulders and neck then rolled down the hill. He followed, jumping on to my chest, pinning my arms and punching both sides of my face. I felt the first shot bounce my head off the grass to the left, the second one to the right, before I managed to yank my arms free and grab his wrists, which I held, white-knuckled, until somebody screamed, 'Teacher.'

Alvin sprang from my chest and shape-shifted into the crowd. The guy holding my glasses put them on my face, pulled me to my feet, told me to run. I stumbled into the pines, still reeling in the thunder, until Mr Evans retrieved me and led me to the principal's office. Swimmy headed, I told Mr Hearty that I thought Sam Stone had offered Alvin money to start the fight. He summoned Stone, told me to go to class. I left the building and walked home.

When Daddy came in from work, he took one look at me and said, 'Don't take an asskickin' again, son. Even if you have to pick up a stick and crack 'em in the head with it.'

I promised that I wouldn't.

That night, lying in bed, staring up into the dark with my face throbbing, I realized that in the two years I'd attended karate class, not once had anyone fought. Not once had anyone made contact with anything solid. Not once had I punched or kicked anything other than a whole lot of air and dreams.

The next day at school, Batman fans and my new friends asked why I hadn't kicked Alvin or punched him back. I shrugged. How could I tell them I didn't know how?

I never returned to fat hairdresser/*Sensei*'s karate class. And it wasn't long after my fight with Alvin that kids at school started calling me Foetus again.

ENTRIES IN MY 1971 Mount Tabor high school annual:

Karate Man, ALIAS Pussyman, ALIAS PIS-ANT,
The karate expert of MTH. Telling all the lies and me
beleiving them. You've made up some good ones. You are
one lieing little sack of shit. I'm glad Lindsor gave you
what was coming to you, you stupid jerkoff.
Rodgers

Fetus,
Who the fuck you think you are? You grew another 1/
100 of a inch this year and 1/16 of a pound. How's
karate? Me and you will have to have a fight sometime.
It's been fun beating Hell out of you in homeroom. Even
when you finally manage to graduate, you're gonna be
nothin but a little turd. Kiss one big rosey red ass, you
future street bum.
Gentle

6

'BRUCE LEE MAY be the world's best-conditioned athle-te', a *Fighting Stars* story announced to movie patrons of North America, 'and its most dynamic living martial artist.'

I know that, I thought. Lee told me so himself, through the lustre of his actions. Tell me something I don't know, like how I can get there, too.

'There are Malaysian tribes who worship him as a god,' Alex Ben Block claimed in a story he wrote for the August 1973 issue of *Esquire*, for sale in stores on 20 July, the date Lee had died. I'd bought a copy of *Esquire* that month when I was bored hanging out with Daddy as he shopped for groceries, but didn't pay much attention to the Lee article until I remembered seeing it after *Enter*.

As soon as I was through with *Fighting Stars*, I pulled the *Esquire* from my socks drawer and read it thoroughly. I learned all sorts of fanboy stuff. Bruce Lee had been born in 1940, the Chinese year of the dragon (I, too, had been born in a year of the dragon, 1952); hence his nickname in Hong Kong, *Li Siu Loong*, 'Small Dragon Lee'. I'd later learn that the dragon is the most powerful, *and* most benevolent, creature in Chinese mythology.

Enter the Dragon was the vehicle designed to introduce Lee to American audiences. He was married; his wife, Linda, was Caucasian-American; they had two children. Lee was Chinese-American (he was one-fourth European, as are Ali and me); he'd studied philosophy at the

University of Washington; had played Kato in *The Green Hornet* TV series (I'd missed him – and maybe enlightenment – because the show was on opposite *The Man from U.N.C.L.E.* in 1966); and Lee 'is too unorthodox to suit most of the conservative karate establishment'.

Block's piece alluded to three movies that Lee had made for Hong Kong audiences; the story had little of the fresh-squeezed martial juice I was hoping for, though its tone suggested such nourishment did exist. It had been designed to tease more than to enlighten, as had *Enter the Dragon* itself. Which would have been great, if Lee hadn't died. But as things were, I found more sustenance in accompanying photographs. (With Lee, one most always finds more in image than anywhere else.)

I cut out the best pictures from both magazines and pasted them to pieces of black construction paper, which I taped to the wall beside the Ali poster opposite my bed, where I'd see them each night before I went to bed and each morning when I woke.

7

IT'S NIGHT. THE moon is round and high.

Someone's standing in front of me. He's naked. His lean golden torso refracts light, breaks it gently and it wavers near him in prisms.

The (first) resurrection of Ali occurred in late 1970. Since I no longer watched TV, Ali existed only as a name I overheard in scraps of conversation: 'that-bull-shittin'-uppity-nigger-Clay', light-haired, fair-skinned country boys spat as I passed them in the halls between classes.

But he seeped back in. Yes. Slowly. Because I felt the bruises Alvin had given me. And I wasn't certain I wanted to, or even could, believe in heroes any more.

I remember a morning near the end of February 1971, about a week after I'd been trounced by Alvin and a few days before the first Ali–Frazier bout. Daddy was driving Carol and me to school and the seven-twenty sports report was on the radio. Ali was being interviewed after a training session. 'The real king is back,' he roared. 'Joe Frazuh ain't nothin' but a pretender to my throne.'

Daddy looked at me, chuckling. 'There's your man,' he said, reaching to turn up the volume. And when he did, Ali's voice rose and rang and punched a hole through the chrome-covered speaker. One thing I'd not forgotten was that voice. The whole time Ali'd been kept from boxing, I'd practised his smoky Southern song in front of mirrors at home and in big-echoing bathrooms at school.

'Joe Frazuh ain't no contest for a scientific boxer like

me. Gowna beat that man *sooo baaddd* about his head and shoulders. Now this might shock and amaze ya, but I'm gowna destroy Joe Frazuh.'

On fight night, although Ali–Frazier was shown live only at closed-circuit locations, on their news programmes all three national TV networks broadcast classic moments from Ali's mid-1960s bouts. Without clips from his fights, I couldn't've comprehended what I'd forgotten. Ali had seemed a fantasy from another time, an impossible and chimerically cheesy myth, like Agent Solo, Superman's invulnerability, or growing up with a healthy, happy and nurturing mom.

How could anyone let six popping punches fly in a single second? *Sensei* had instructed us to always throw only one blow and to deliver it only from the rear arm. Only the rear arm had any true power in it. Yet right in front of my eyes Ali was doing it, punching real, live human beings with near-invisible speed with both hands. And he punched effortlessly and seemed *never* to miss, gliding about the ring as gracefully as panther-like karate masters fat *Sensei* had imagined. Here he was on my TV screen, Muhammad Ali, the Black Superman, so much more than my shadowy memories of him.

That night, I went to bed with my transistor radio tucked under my pillow. I pulled it out, tugged the stiff leather strap up around my wrist, placed the leather-covered speaker against my ear, and spun the tiny plastic dial back and forth until I found an announcer who was summarizing each round of the fight after it had been fought. A little after midnight he said Frazier had won a decision. Although I didn't believe him, I wept.

Within days, Ali made me feel better when he told the world he hadn't really lost. 'Hit Joe Frazuh six times for every time he hit me. Joe Frazuh stayed in the hospital for two weeks after the fight. *Maannn*, I sent Joe Frazuh to the hospital for two solid weeks.'

So. I found myself standing in front of mirrors around the house again, flipping my wormy left arm towards the reflection, trying to replicate Ali's hot and sweet snake-lick jab. My romance with martial art returned and I began to work on variations of some basic karate hand strikes, applying what I could understand of Ali's boxing style to help loosen up the stiff Japanese techniques. I practised *Sansen-tsuki*, which translates as 'fighting blow', the first punch karate beginners are taught. *Sansen-tsuki* is thrown from the full-frontal *hachiji-dachi* position, fists inverted and on the waist, knees bent and legs spread as if you're trying to strapple a set of railroad tracks.

Instead of keeping my fists closed tight as *Sensei* had taught, I held my hands loose and open ever so slightly, like Ali's. I turned to the left to present a smaller target, tucked my chin in low next to my shoulder, raised my right hand to ear level, dangled the left one at my side (jabs can be popped loose and snappy and much faster from waist height), stationed my legs a couple feet apart and bent them just a little at the knees. Behind my heat-seeking jab, I worked on slinging as many twisting *Sansen-tsuki* as I could in two seconds, concentrating on throwing punches not in rote patterns like *Sensei*, but in unpredictable rhythms and groupings.

Throughout the spring of 1971 I practised my punches about three days out of every seven, but then, since I longed to be accepted by other Mount Tabor guys (most of whom thought that the coolest of the cool, the real men, were ones who stayed drunk half the time), I caught a case of teenage dipsomania.

That summer I drank and drank, until I built up enough tolerance to down a daily six-pack of Miller Malt Liquor, wanting people to associate the famous name with my own. All the eighty-pound, nineteen-year-old drunks I've known are fairly incapable of organized, rapid, sustained, physical activity. Instead of training to become more like Ali, I settled for a tentative flick or two from my left fist every time I passed a mirror.

I began smoking cigars, fat ole stogies nearly twice as big around as my thumb. I didn't inhale the smoke, just sucked it in and blew it out, the cigar hanging out of the corner of my mouth, my left arm hooked around a rolled-down car window, trying to look cool perched up high on the seat cushion I needed to see over the steering wheel, even as discharged smoke found its stinging way into my eyes. I bought cigars in ten-cent packs of six that barely fit into the starched pockets of my boys' size 12 shirts. And I completed my look by wearing English-style Ben Hogan golf caps at the accepted cool Southern angle, brim high and slightly to the left of my nose, cap tilted fifteen degrees left of level.

I tried to join the Polish Drinking Team, a fraternal and elitist group of ballplayers and wrestlers founded and led by Frank Romanosky and Ken Wesolowsky, both of whom had been born to Russian parents. Romo and Weso were renowned for borrowing Weso's old man's bulldog's collar and leash and leading each other around on all fours, barking and growling at women in the halls, at bars, and in fast-food places.

Fetus, glad you didn't make it to the PDT, you godamed pussy. It sure would be nice to anitiate your scrawny little ass anyway.
Arfmann(ski)

All through my high school years, I took two to three showers every day; each time I passed a sink I scrubbed my hands, which became pink, then chapped, then scaly. I washed my hair nightly and, when I stepped from the shower, left it dripping wet, soaking it further with a fifth-can of hair spray, combing out the curls I'd inherited from my mother, then letting it dry helmet-hard and sleeping on it. First thing in the mornings, I spent a quarter of an hour brushing out the crusty spray. And hoped I looked straight and normal like other guys at school.

I bought clothes with every cent of my allowance I hadn't committed to beer and cigars. I owned probably two dozen sweaters (boys' size 14) and pairs of trousers (14 slim) and twice that many shirts. The clothes hangers in my closet were equidistantly spaced. Long-sleeved shirts were organized by colours and were separated from short sleeves and from trousers. Ten or so golf caps were stored side by side on the high shelf of the closet; each day of the week I'd hide my hair under a different colour cap. My closet floor was lined with pair after pair of (size $4\frac{1}{2}$) dress shoes. At night, when I took off the shoes I'd worn that day, I'd polish them until they gleamed more brightly than brand-new. Trousers were professionally dry-cleaned and pressed, I never wore jeans or T-shirts, and I'd not put on a shirt that didn't have about ten pounds of starch in it. I felt a need to remain not only crisp but spotless. Unsoiled. Clean, every moment.

In early July, before my senior year, Daddy bought a three-year-old, turquoise, 327/four-barrel Camaro that sported its original tyres and only 12,000 on the odometer. 'Would want one of these if I was your age, son,' he said, passing me the keys. On his small salary as a foreman in a plant that made corrugated boxes in which cartons of R.J. Reynolds cigarettes were packed, Daddy couldn't afford such an expensive car. I knew he'd bought it to make me feel better, to help me find a life. And I was grateful – or as grateful as anyone can be when he's dead asleep. I promised Daddy I'd take special care of the car.

The rest of that summer and through the fall, I washed the Camaro twice a week, every week, spent an hour or so cleaning the interior each time it was washed, and I waxed it every second week. Its black vinyl interior always shone. The turquoise paint beaded water better than anybody else's car I knew. At night, even when it wasn't raining, the Camaro looked wet with city lights and polyurethane. Everybody wanted to ride in my Camaro. Even ones who didn't like me. And I didn't mind giving people rides. But I didn't let anybody use the ashtrays and everyone had to wipe their feet before placing them on the floor mats. At least I pretended I could make them do those things.

That summer, I'd had my biggest growth spurt ever. I got all the way to five-foot-three, and even broke eighty pounds. But in the fall few people noticed. I still needed my seat cushion to see over the steering wheel.

The second Friday of October, Weso and Romo asked me for a ride to the football game so they could get good and juiced without worrying which of them would drive. I thought football was the dumbest sport going, all those fat-asses standing out in the light for everybody to see, wearing all those fat-ass pads and stupid uniforms and helmets and a ball and rules and shit. But everybody at Mount Tabor went to the games. And, man, did I want to be like everybody else.

The night before the game, we made a couple gallons of Purple Jesus and stored it in the trunk of the Camaro. Staring out the window in geometry, I could see it patiently waiting for us, ripening and getting devoutly toxic.

I washed and waxed the Camaro after school and spent two dollars filling up with petrol. It was grey and cold that Friday and clouds were round and silver and rolling like ones you'd expect to see in *Jason and the Argonauts* or *The Ten Commandments*. Just the right clouds and weather for football, even if I did hate the stupid goddamn sport.

When I was ready to leave the house around six-thirty, every detail looked right for a fine Friday night. I slipped my fingers around the steering wheel, patted the accelerator, turned the key in the ignition, and felt the engine hum all the way from my fingers to my toes. I slid my Stylistics tape into the 8-track, popped the transmission into first and purred on down the road, getting off on my sweet soft soul sounds and admiring the street-light reflections on my fresh-waxed hood.

I picked up the two self-proclaimed Polacks and tooled on over in the direction of the stadium. They were both dipping deep into the vat of PJ and were pretty wasted before we got to the game. We parked the car and moved off behind the stadium, away from the lights and into a stand of scraggly pines and dogwoods. The patch of woods was cold. The smell of wet fallen leaves enveloped us. We quickly found a place where we couldn't see the parking lot; bunches of ground-out cigarette butts were at the base of the fence. When I'd climbed halfway, I noticed Romo wasn't with us. I turned and looked for him and couldn't see through the trees. I jumped from the fence and stepped out from the woods into salmon-pink light from the big fluorescents.

There he was, about fifty yards from the Camaro, in the middle of a shining circle of shattered glass where nobody'd parked. Around him stood a gaggle of ten or so chest-high, maybe thirteen-year-old black kids. And Romanosky was in a sort of pseudo-*kiba-dachi* stance, right fist fully extended at shoulder height, the other inverted on the hip. And he was making some kind of dumb squealing noise and was hopping up and down like a radioactive rooster.

I sprinted across the parking lot to help. After all, if anybody understood blacks, it was me. I dressed black, walked black, talked black. Ali was my man, Miss Rapley was the coolest person I'd ever met and I was the Mount Tabor High king of soul music.

As I ran toward Romo, I heard Weso's big feet clunking up behind. I made it there first, even with my short-ass legs.

'Hey, cuz, what's goin' on?' I asked the tallest and blackest and oiliest of the kids, the one as big as me who seemed to be the leader.

He ignored me. 'Here comes your white-ass cavalry, Mister Karate Man,' he said to Romo, sporting the coldest grin I had ever seen. We were only a few miles south of the downtown R.J. Reynolds plants. The sweet, over-ripe smell of pissgold broadleaf was on the air. I pulled at Frank's sleeve. His longish cheeks looked tight and sunken. One of them trembled every few seconds. It was cold enough to see his breath in the air; his reddish hair was stuck by sweat to his temples; his skin looked clammy.

'Come on, Romo, let's go,' I said. 'Come on, now, don't nobody want no trouble.' I felt glass crunch under my shoes.

And Crowblack hit me on the stomach with a bag of nickels he'd been hiding somewhere. I heard it jangle and figured what it was. But it didn't hurt. I guess he didn't know how to angle a punch.

Why'd you do that? I wanted to ask. Look at my clothes. Hear my voice. Go to my ride, check out the sounds I listen to. Can't you tell how hip I am? Don't look at my face. That ain't me. Can't you tell I'm a lot like you? Can't you see these clowns use me, too?

And Crowblack tried to hit me again. That's when I had the Ali flashback. Crowblack's chin appeared like a lighted window in a darkened wall. Everything else disappeared.

Before he got his bag-slow fist halfway around, I stabbed him, flat on the bridge of the nose, with two hard left jabs. Just like the ones Ali'd impaled Cleveland Williams on. Where had those come from? I'd only imagined *Ali* throwing the punches. If I'd thought about *me* doing it, I would've gotten scared and wouldn't've been able to.

The blows had come out so smooth and easy, just like The Champ's. And then Crowblack was lying down. And there was blood everywhere; everywhere there was blood. From out of his nostrils, around his mouth, down his chin and holey white T-shirt, it flowed. There was a small puddle of it on the asphalt and glass beside his head.

I looked for Weso: he was running for the car. Romo stood kind of beside me, off to the left, in that stupid *kiba-dachi* someone had shown him. 'Go ahead,' another black kid was saying, 'try some of your ka-raw-ti-shit.' No one knew that I'd hit Crowblack.

I grabbed Romo by the arm and pulled him hard, spinning him towards me. 'The car,' I said, 'go to the car,' and I dug my feet in and took off running. Frank beat me to the Camaro and I threw him the keys. He unlocked the door on the passenger's side and he and Weso slid together on to the bucket seat. One of them opened my door for me.

I jumped in behind the wheel, we locked both doors and tried to rip out of there. A big black Buick pulled in the way and blocked the exit. Another dark car fell in behind.

I couldn't back up, couldn't go forward. There I sat with my foot on the brake while the hive of dirty, sweaty, thirteen-year-olds descended on my cleanmeancoolblue ride. They swarmed all around, whirling up and down on the fenders, smearing street-soiled fingers all over my fresh-Windexed windows. And then Crowblack was there, blood pouring from his nose, green shining shards of glass sticking out of his cheek, standing beside my door. And he had an almost empty Rebel Yell bottle coiled in his fist, the bottle not yet a part of the hand, his hand still young and mouldable-looking, looking like it should be holding a couple slices of Sunbeam bread with peanut butter chunked up in between.

He swung and broke the bottle on the window next to my face. I jumped and got both hands up beside my head, but the window didn't shatter. Weso or Romo or both of them yelled, 'There's some cops, over there.'

I looked where they pointed. Not a hundred yards away, there they were, two of them, both white, directing traffic with big orange flashlights, looking bored as the kids in remedial English class. I blew the horn once, twice, held it down. Crowblack was kicking my door. Two other kids were pounding on the hood. One cop looked up, said something at his partner, pulled out his stick and jogged methodically towards us. I saw a lot of legs dart past, turned and watched thirteen-year-olds fly off in some ten different trajectories.

The Buick in front of us finally moved. I pulled on to the street, over to the kerb, climbed out and told my story to the second cop. He looked sleepy and kept directing traffic.

'Well, what do you expect me to do, son?' he said in his best dismissive cop voice. 'Something like this happens most every weekend.'

Yeah, I thought, but you're missing the point. The point is it doesn't happen to me and my Camaro – and you're not a very nice guy to be a peace officer. 'Look at these giant dents all over my car,' is all I said.

'Go on about your business, son,' he answered.

To calm down, we drove around a while, each taking a couple dips into the vat of PJ. When we figured the game was over, we headed for Staley's, a burger joint that had been the post-game hangout for at least a thousand years.

About halfway there, Weso clapped me on the shoulder. 'Goddamn, Davis, didn't know you had it in you,' he said. 'You know, you've gotten real good at that judo stuff.'

I smiled and pushed my golf cap further back from my brow. He'd called me 'Davis'. I couldn't remember the last time anybody'd called me by my name, except my father and sister. To everybody else I was Foetus, or Runt, or Mouse, or Shrimp, or Tadpole, or Pissant, or something besides me.

'What belt you got now, anyway, a black?'

I didn't say that what I'd done wasn't any kind of Asian martial art. Or that it had happened mostly by accident. And that if it had anything to do with anybody, my mentor was Ali. I just kept on smiling and driving.

In celebration of my act of good ole boy heroism, I was admitted to the Polish Drinking Team. Romo and Weso presented me with a jersey at a special meeting at the hospitality room of the Schlitz brewery out off Highway 109. The shirt was royal blue; my name and title had been stencilled on in big yellow block letters above my official number, '00'. Royal blue and yellow: the Mount Tabor colours. The shirt read 'PISSANT-SKI, DRILL INSTRUCTOR'. I tried it on. It was only a million sizes too big.

Every Friday, I proudly wore the jersey as if it were a letter sweater – I had my starched shirt on underneath. PDT meetings took place on Friday nights at Sam's Tavern on the Green. Soon it was February and time to order caps and gowns. A form was given to seniors requesting correct spelling of names for graduation programmes. I printed mine as, 'Davis Worth Miller', then added 'the third', which, of course, was a lie. But I thought it made me sound cool, made me special.

In the area provided for honours and activities, I listed

myself as Drill Instructor for the Polish Jerkoff Team, Alvin Lindsor's sparring partner, and charter member of Detention Study Hall. When Daddy asked to attend my graduation, I told him I'd decided not to go. But I didn't tell a single person at school.

That fall, everybody enrolled in college, or got a job, or joined the military and ended up in Vietnam. I didn't do any of those things. Every day, first thing when I woke, I'd pull the Camaro out of the driveway and head for Highway 158. If it was lunchtime, I'd hear the twelve-thirty freight moaning up ahead and I'd go left, following the sound and the tracks up The Strip, past tobacco and cotton and corn fields, vegetable stands and feed stores, thundering around old slow-going Ford and Chevy pickups, up where 158 becomes Stratford Road and kudzu vines stop creeping so close to the road and you can't smell them any more when they die in the fall, past the spots where white kids cruise on weekend nights – Putt-Putt, where I'd sometimes pass the train, and McDonald's and the Triangle Drive-In – and on into town, right on by Krispy Kreme's shining green and red neon sign imperatively flashing *Hot Doughnuts NOW* as if the words meant something, and past fat-ass Lincolns and Cadillacs parked at Food Fair and at Davis Department Store over at Thruway and the old women who drove the Caddies and who struggled to open and close their fat-ass car doors.

Don't none of the people in this town know nothin' about nothin', I'd think, and they don't want to know nothin'. But I don't know nothin' either, and don't have nowhere to go, and don't know how to get there if I did.

Until it turned cold that fall, I'd lie in the sun and suck beer and listen to Isaac Hayes 8-tracks. I'd walk down to Silas Creek and stare at the water and try to imagine me and some girl (any girl) in rolled-up jeans splashing about just like in Salem cigarette ads. And when I went back inside, I did the old funky strut in front of the mirrors, angling my body as if I was one bad stud midnight Ali/ black motherfucker. If Carol walked past while I was at the mirrors, I'd zing a couple fast jabs a half-inch from her face to run her ass off.

Around four o'clock, I'd start preening to go out. Just before time for Daddy to get home, I'd steal a few dollars from the top drawer of his bureau and leave the house. I'd buy a couple sixes of Miller Malt and maybe a Zero bar or packet of Saltines and a box of Swisher Sweet cigars for dessert, then take the Camaro up to Sherwood Forest Elementary, the school I'd been going to when my mother died, where I'd push my Stylistics tape into the player – 'Betcha by golly, wow', the disembodied voices would croon, 'You're the one that I've been waiting for' – and there I'd sit in the parking lot and pretend to talk to my own personal specialprivateladyfriend, tell her all the secrets I didn't have but desperately felt I needed to talk about.

I'm on the playground. Riding the roundabout. I lay my head way back and watch clouds roll around me. I get dizzy. I look down. And she's there, naked and wet, like she stepped from a stream, and she'd standing in front of the pines. Her hair flows down the sides of her face. The roundabout stops. I stare. Her skin is luminous with water and suntan and ancestry. She's standing, legs apart, hands on her lips, waiting for me. Standing like girls in Playboy. *Beads of water reflect light from the V of black hair down there. I step off the roundabout. My mouth feels numb. I run my tongue across my gums. I don't feel any teeth. I reach in: they all fall out. I see them lying in the sand. I look up. And she's gone.*

By late October I was so frustrated I'd run down the hill,

past the swings and the roundabout and the sandbox, down to the centre of the baseball field, and I'd peer down at Daddy's house, nestled deep inside its noiselessness, and I'd think about him and Carol sitting there watching Andy Griffith on TV. And I'd walk in one great circle for a time before I'd stop and, in the monochromatic light from the fat moon, I'd snatch my hat from my head and fling it out across the sand, pull heavy-starched shirt and razor-creased trousers from my body and crumple them into knots and slam them in the dust and I'd run, reed-thin white and naked, glowing ghostlike under the moon, through grey brittle frost-laden crab grass and I'd snort the air and smoke it out in silver ice clouds and I'd smash empty beer bottles against rough pine bleachers and I'd take my left hand, curl my fingers towards my palm, squeezing my nails hard into the flesh like *Sensei* had taught, ball up my fist stiff as a mace, and I'd hit myself again and again and again, on my belly, my abdomen, my legs, until I went first red then purple and I'd hit myself some more.

I wanted it to hurt, bad, but I never seemed to feel the pain and, even if I did, I still hadn't hurt myself bad enough to make me feel better, so I'd put my trousers back on and my shirt and I'd find my cap and climb back up the hill, trying to smooth out wrinkles as best I could. And I'd drive home and it'd be two or three in the morning and I'd sneak in the last couple beers, take a seat in the den, turn on the television and drink and sob silently until I lost myself in the familiar steady drone of the post-sign-off test pattern.

Not knowing anything I wanted, but figuring I had to do something before Daddy booted me out of the house, I started college on 23 August 1973. It was less than five months before my twenty-second birthday. I'd reached my full adult height, five-foot-seven, and I weighed ninety pounds. I'd never become the greatest heavyweight champion of all time, but at least I was too skinny to be sent to Vietnam. What's more, I'd finally got tall enough to not use a seat cushion to drive.

8

NOT FIVE DAYS after having met Bruce Lee in *Enter the Dragon*, I found an article written by the man himself, found in it a wisdom alive and new and China to me (and, beyond China, the *world*!), among mouldering, sweet-smelling stacks of magazines in the basement of the Lees-McRae Junior College library in Banner Elk, North Carolina, USA.

The title: 'Liberate Yourself from Classical Karate'.

Accompanying the article were three black-and-white photos of Lee sparring with a robot-looking-type, into whose head and body were being chunked punches and kicks rocketed from impossible-seeming angles. Impossible in that I'd seen no one else who could've conceived of them, much less done them.

These photos were not movie-still glossies, but images of techniques as real as Lee's brick-hard fists; fists sheathed, in the photos, by thickly padded boxing gloves.

Lee's partner had on Everlast boxing headgear. Despite the protection, the partner's features were being contorted by the impact of Lee's blows. And once again: you could see it, even in these frozen glimpses, boiling up from Lee's insides, the Power, affecting the catcher in waves, the sparring 'partner', the heavy bag with legs. Both men were working out in sweat clothes and tennis shoes. Lee wasn't wearing a shirt and he was bouncing about on the balls of his feet, like a boxer. His skin refracted southern California sun.

'Classical karate' types (*Sensei* and the *karatekas* I'd seen in martial arts magazines) would never have posed for photographs, or even worked out, in such attire. They would've been decked out in starched white uniforms and full black-belt drag, driving stakes through boards with their foreheads or allowing themselves to be run over by half-ton Toyota flatbeds.

I studied the pictures a long, awed time before I read the words. And was not disappointed when I got to the body of the story.

'I am concerned with the blossoming of a martial artist,' Lee wrote, 'not a Chinese martial artist or a Japanese martial artist. A martial artist is a human being first. As nationalities have nothing to do with one's (basic) humanity, so they have nothing to do with martial art.

'Leave all preconceptions behind,' Lee said. 'Leave your protective shell of isolation,' he told me, 'and relate *directly* to what is being said.'

Foetus, he was calling, *come out, come out, wherever you are.*

'Fighting, as is, is simple and total,' Lee continued. 'It is not limited to your perspective or conditioning as a Chinese or Korean martial artist. True observation begins when one sheds set patterns, and true freedom of expression occurs when one is beyond systems. Regardless of their many colourful origins (by a wise, mysterious monk, by a special messenger in a dream, or in a holy revelation), styles are created by men. A style should not be considered gospel truth ... Man, the living, creating individual, is always more important than any style.'

In that moment, for the first time ever, I wasn't nothing. It no longer bothered me not to be just like other kids. For the first time I felt like something and that something (someone!) had been named. There was nothing wrong with being different. Being different could mean being an individual. I was an *individual*! Or at least I could become one. When I began living.

'At best, styles are parts dissected from a whole. Divisive by nature, styles keep men apart rather than unite them.'

Lee was referring specifically to systems of martial art: tae kwon do, karate, kung fu, judo, kendo, but I took the term (and Lee's article) allegorically, to apply to any conditioning, any training, any capsulization, any categorization, any habit. 'Style' could mean religiosity, ethnicity, any prejudice. It might mean 'lifestyle' or any other *way* of thinking or being. It could mean idealizing a person, notion or situation; it could mean regarding one region of the world, or people who live there, as being better than another. It might mean making a big fucking deal out of Christmas or a stupid fucking football team or using 'good' goddamn table manners or most any ole construct. It might even mean feeling that to make it through the day you need a clean, mean ride with a full tank of gas and have to wear snazzy trousers and hard-starched shirts.

Then. It began seeming like one tiny dumb joke, finally; all of it. Everything I'd perpetrated on myself for half my life. Wallowing in the romance of sorrow, in the joy of melancholy. Blaming my lot on my mother's death, on God, on people, on the world. I'd closed myself off to almost everyone and everything around me and to myself, although I stayed so deeply inside of me. Inside of me in pretty unfortunate ways.

I'll not do it any longer, I declared right at that moment. I choose not to frame myself, not to encapsulate myself, not to 'live' in a shell any longer. Nor will I adopt a 'lifestyle', choose somebody else's way, to replace my shell. I'll not join anybody's colony; not select a side; choose neither to believe nor to disbelieve; not step along; not be a passenger.

I choose, instead, to live a life. Foetus will punch and kick his way out of his shell.

'Look around the martial arts,' Lee continued, 'and witness the assortment of routine performers, trick artists, desensitized robots, glorifiers of the past. *Life is constant movement* – rhythmic as well as random. Life is continual change, not stagnation. Instead of choicelessly flowing with this process of change, many "masters", past and present, rigidly subscribe to traditional concepts and techniques of the art, solidifying the everflowing, dissecting the totality.'

I finally saw my own Japanese/Negroese isolationist rituals for what they were, then. At best, I'd chosen to 'live' parts of the *LIFE* available to me, to limit my experiences, to solidify the everflowing, to choose the security of my cage, to settle for a niche, over the vast, vast world open to us.

'Lacking boundaries,' Lee wrote, 'combat is always fresh, alive, constantly changing. Consider the subtle difference between having no form and having no-form. The first is ignorance; the second, transcendence. Through instinctive body feeling' – *Foetus, get back to what you once were*, he was saying, *what you are* – 'each of us *knows* our own most efficient and dynamic manner of achieving leverage, balance in motion, economic use of energy. Patterns, techniques and forms touch only the fringe of understanding.'

These were ideas (non-ideas?) I'd not previously heard. 'These paragraphs are, at best, a finger pointing to the moon,' Lee concluded. 'Do not take the finger to be the moon or fix your gaze so intently on the finger as to miss the beautiful sights of heaven.'

He'd used similar lines in *Enter*. I'd not understood them when I saw the movie. Reading 'Liberate Yourself from Classical Karate', I felt that I did. I admired his presumptive non-presumptiveness, his pretentious nonpretentiousness. But what struck me most was the implied belief that people should have a grace, a fluidity, of personality and of thought and of movement. To have less is to be not quite human, not quite alive.

Lee intimated that these properties are innate – and that we've forgotten them. Most importantly, his body stated in movement, these attributes can be recovered and honed. 'Yes,' I said aloud. A rounder, cosmic *Yes!!* roared up from my gut.

Over the next few weeks, I ordered numerous back issues of martial arts magazines with articles about or by Lee and looked up every account I could find of his death, not only from Lees-McRae but twenty miles down the Blue Ridge in Boone at Appalachian State University's library.

'Kung-fu movie star', most newspaper articles categorized him as. At first I cared what they called Lee, then I quit caring what they said and quit reading their easy obits, though I was mystified by the lack of real writing about the man – this meteoric, snapshot brief presence – his death and his *life*.

9

THE FIRST TIME anyone called me smart, other than my father, it happened at Lees-McRae. The person who thought I was smart was Karen Barefoot, my freshman composition teacher.

Like me, it was Karen's first year at Lees-McRae. She was born in Charlotte and had taught at a university in Melbourne, Australia. While there, she wrote and (unsuccessfully) submitted short fiction to magazines in the US. When she got the hankering to come back to North Carolina, she chose Lees-McRae because, she said, 'it seemed like the right environment to do serious work'.

And Lees-McRae's campus did look like a 'serious' place. The Old Worldish white stone buildings seemed to have been carved from the very ribs of the mountain on which they'd been erected, and furniture in those buildings hand-hewn from ancient wind-gnarled reptilian-trunk cedar and hemlock forests that adorned nearby Beech and Sugar Mountains' regal bodies – forests whose rising, glowing morning mists, tinted by pigments in the needles, give the Blue Ridge chain its name. All in all, a postcard-perfect setting for a small campus.

Of course, academic-seeming cosmetics aren't why I went to Lees-McRae. I could tell you I chose the school because it was small (560 students) and because area ski resorts looked like places James Bond should hang out. But the real reason I landed at 'Lose-McRae', as we students called it, is that it was the only school with standards crummy enough for folks in its admissions office to give me a chance. And even then, they decided I'd be on academic probation for my first year.

In the fourteen months since high school, I'd begun to grow up and get more sophisticated. I'm sure this is true because at Lees-McRae I learned to lie better than in high school. Or at least more profitably. I became an 'A' student, not because I was studious, but because I learned to appear bright. Which isn't too tough, when you're as geeky-looking as me.

The class I most enjoyed was Karen's. I liked it because she encouraged students to call her Karen, because she didn't mind if we didn't come to lectures 'as long as you find something worthwhile to do', because she taught by telling stories, because she let us write about what we wanted (the more personal the better), and because she was a stone fox. I began to write pseudo-seriously because Karen believed I was good at it and wasn't shy about saying so. And if it would please Karen, well, I'd just become the greatest writer of all times.

Karen was lean and tall and her hair was alive and dark and long. She wore it French-braided on the sides like Olivia Hussey had in a couple scenes in Franco Zeffirelli's *Romeo and Juliet*, which Karen showed in class before we read the play. Karen wore round wire-rimmed glasses and jeans and peasant tops or thin sundresses. And as she stood in streaming shafts of sun at the front of class, reading one or another of her favourite passages from books she'd assigned, standing in filtered sunlight speaking in her slow and sultry Southern melody, it wasn't at all hard to tell that Karen wore no underwear.

In class I stared at Karen, usually forgetting to listen to what she said. But I gobbled up the books she assigned: Edith Hamilton's *Classical Mythology*; Shakespeare's *A Midsummer Night's Dream*; *Lord Jim*; *Light in August*;

Of Mice and Men; *The Old Man and the Sea*; *The Great Gatsby*. The only book Karen asked us to read that I couldn't get through was *Catcher in the Rye*. Who has time to listen to some juvenile maladjust whine pointlessly for a couple hundred pages, except somebody who wishes the world would suffer their whine? God, there's got to be something in the world beyond pointless adolescent whining.

And Karen Barefoot showed me a bit of it: I started getting off on rhythms of good writing. After class, back in my dorm room, I could enter worlds Karen had shown me – lands of gods, goddesses and heroes, and of men with lives so orderly their essences could be caught on paper. The coolest line I remember Karen quoting in class was by the Roman playwright Terence. That old slave, born about a hundred years before Jesus, said the most amazing thing. 'I am human, and nothing human is foreign to me,' he said. I wish I'd known to say the same thing about myself.

My favourite character in Karen's books was Gatsby. Ole James Gatz was awfully slick for an Anglo-Saxon. I admired his monogrammed shirts; white, pink and yellow linen suits; sleek fast cars and most of the rest of his style.

It was mostly because I was pretentious enough to see some irony of Gatz's life in my own, that and the knife-on-bare-skin cold mountain autumn, that I loosened up and started wearing clothes that were a little less uptown. Not to imply I would've gone so far as to don a pair of Levis or a coloured T-shirt or tennis shoes or even would've left the top button of a shirt undone. And there's no way I would've taken off my thin alpaca sweaters and golf caps. I'm saying only that practical winter garb was a necessity in the mountains and the fall of 1973 was one of the coldest on record. And that my closet at school was filled, by Daddy's graciousness, with corduroys and flannels in most of the rich bright colours of the rainbow.

In my room, I could stand in front of the little mirror over the small pine dresser in the furthest corner and toss blow after blow at the reflection in the glass – five jabs from a side stance, pivot to the front and rivet the air with four quick *sansen-tsuki*, back to the jab and up on my toes, bouncing from side to side, popping the air with blows, dancing to my left and away from the mirror, thinking of the reflected face and body as that of Frazier or *Sensei*, or black-garbed Ninja assassins I'd read about in the library, or Tom Buchanan in *Gatsby*, or the jokish assholes I imagined going out with all the fine-looking women I was interested in. Sometimes, when I was slinging punches, I even got so worked up I took my cigar out of my mouth and left it in an ashtray on the desk. I didn't know how to throw a right hand and didn't see much purpose for the blow, what with my well-reared snake of a left jab being so fast and deadly and all.

To impress Karen Barefoot, I wrote 'autobiographical' stories about having been born in Korea during the war and having studied tae kwon do from the age of five. I fashioned long, self-piteous 'poems' (stolen from sappy pop songs by Bread and Dan Fogelberg) about being young, brilliant and absolutely misunderstood by everyone around me. And I wrote about Ali. The only 'Bs' I got from Karen were for my Ali stories. I thought the Ali papers were pretty good.

When I wrote about Ali and boxing and karate, I worked hard at being knowledgeable. I went to the library and looked up magazine articles about Ali and any of the martial arts and read, then reread them; slowly, carefully, then read them yet again. More than read, I *internalized* the magazine pieces and didn't care if they were sloppily written.

Another cool thing began happening, too: even though

I wasn't intending to learn anything, a number of my classes became fun. And, because they were fun, I found myself starting to learn.

In addition to Karen, I had one other very good teacher at Lees-McRae. Mr Wilson, who taught religions of the world, was lots different from frumpy, twangy-tongued old disciplinarians at Mount Tabor. Mr Wilson was tall, thin and probably about fifty, though he had few wrinkles. If his hair hadn't been grey, you would've thought he was maybe thirty-five.

Every day he wore a different corduroy shirt, tan khaki trousers, and the same pair of always new-looking brown work boots. He spoke softly, simply, carefully; he wore his shirts open-collared, and most times, even when caught unawares, he had a slight smile and look of great discovery on his face.

About three weeks into the semester and two weeks before I found Bruce Lee, on the day we were to review for our first exam, the one on Hinduism and Buddhism, Mr Wilson arrived for class ten minutes late. He placed his books on the desk and said, 'Before we start, I want to tell you about the Chinese idea of the Superior Man.'

A wave of groans rolled about the room. Mr Wilson chuckled. 'Don't worry,' he said, 'you won't be responsible for it on the test.'

He pulled out his chair, spun it around, straddled it and took a seat, his arms draped over the barred back. 'The Bible tells us we're born evil,' he said, 'but Asian philosophers say there are no such things as good and evil. Things and people are simply what they are and can't be judged as right or wrong, good and bad.'

He paused, placing his right palm under his chin and leaned forward on the chair-back, giving us a moment to consider what he'd said. 'And you know what else? Taoists, Buddhists and Confucians *all* teach that there is such a person as "the Superior Man". Turn to page 174

in your books, where we'll look for "the Superior Man"
... Ah, here he is – halfway down the page, end of the
third paragraph. Read the lines in quotation marks for
us, will you, please, Nancy?'

Nancy Blevins's voice rose from the rear of the room:
' "The way of the Superior Man is that of an empty
vessel. It is easier to carry than a full one." '

Mr Wilson closed his book. 'Thanks, Nancy. OK, let's
begin our review.'

Wow. What a mind- and gut-tease. Here was a concept
I could half-relate to, my Superman fantasies not long
past. After class, I skipped maths, went to my room, and
read the chapter on Chinese philosophies, all four pages
of it, in the 409-page text. The only mention of the
Superior Man was those lines on page 174, offered as an
example of a Chinese proverb.

I headed for the library and, after searching for an
hour, found one thin book called *Chinese Proverbial
Wisdom*, the author of which was a real Chinese-sound-
ing sort named Shapiro. The Superior Man was men-
tioned twice.

> *MEDITATION 42*
> *The Superior Man is as water –*
> *reach for him, he cannot be held.*

> *MEDITATION 58*
> *The Superior Man*
> *when he walks alone*
> *is without fear.*
> *If he must renounce society*
> *it does not matter.*

I left the library feeling perplexed *and* kind of excited.

10

I READ REVIEWS of *Enter the Dragon* and was surprised
that most were favourable. 'Bruce Lee's performance is
fascinating,' the reviewer for *Time* magazine wrote. 'Lee
died recently in Hong Kong under mysterious circumstances.
He could not be more alive than here.'

I wrote my own *Enter* review for the *Fountainhead*,
Lees-McRae's student newspaper. I can't pretend my
piece was good; editors would've taken most anything to
fill space with student copy. The paper typically used
Associated Press stuff for filler.

I began shadow-boxing regularly, late at night, in the
hall outside my room. I concentrated on lateral movement (not easy to do in a hallway) and on throwing quick
relaxed kicks, not having learned to kick even moderately
well from fat *Sensei*, who could barely raise a foot above
knee height. I began popping kicks loose and snappy and
soon found a freedom accompanying each one thrown.

'Hey, when you gonna make that movie?' guys kidded
when I was out in the hall flicking kicks. '*Enter the
Foetus*, right?' And they'd chuckle. 'Or is it *The Foetal
Connection*?' And I'd startle myself by laughing. Because
it was funny. A lot of things had recently become funny.

Dancing in front of the mirror in my room. Listening to
the Marvin Gaye tune, 'Distant Lover'. Wanting to be as
fluid in movement as Gaye's voice.

Wrapping the melody around me. Trying to become

the song, thinking I might learn a little about what it would be to have a distant lover. Emulating the *Soul Train* dancers. I can perform most all of their moves and even work basic karate techniques into my dance, creating a couple movements I can call my own.

While dancing, working to throw a front-kick while moving laterally, not like the 'kick' on page eleven of Masutaku Oyama's *Best Karate*, with which Oyama claims to have killed 800-lb bulls; Oyama's technique is slow, stiff, predictable, more push than kick and altogether impractical.

My left trouser leg slaps against itself as I bring my kick alive, throwing it slick and slippery. *Ftwuu* is the sound the kick makes as it comes in combinations – up from the floor and out to waist height, chest height, head height; head, chest, waist, groin. Fifty times, one hundred, two hundred times, on the beat, the half-beat, the quarter-beat.

It's night, the moon is round and high. Someone's standing in front of me. He's naked. His lean golden torso refracts light, breaks it gently and it wavers near him in prisms. At first I don't know this man. Then I see that he is me.

At midterm, I had 'As' in Mr Wilson's, in Karen's, in biology, and in Western civilization, the first 'good' grades I'd made since my mother died, though I didn't much care what my grades were. I'd learned from Lee not only not to care about grades, but to not-care about them in a brand-new (non)way. In classes I didn't study or take notes. I simply listened carefully to what instructors said and thought about what the words meant. I was beginning to have confidence in my brightness, having been helped by Lee to recognize that I wasn't stupid – and that lots of other 'stupid' people aren't, either. I'd affected that pose, that 'form', in high school in the hope of becoming popular.

I dropped algebra in mid-October; the stuff didn't strike me as any more practical than *Sensei*'s stupid strikes and stances. Why weren't we shown how to count change, how to add and subtract without using pen and paper, compute our gas mileage, do income taxes, how to cleanly, beautifully snap a left jab, say 'Please' and 'Thank you' and 'Yes, sir' and 'No, ma'am', or something, anything, we might be able to use at some point in our lives? All this robot-maths stuff could use a dose of Bruce Lee real-world revamping.

At the beginning of the ten-day midterm break, when other guys drove to Florida or Myrtle Beach in groups, I drove the eighty-nine miles to Daddy's house alone. This was nothing new: out of pure boredom, I'd driven to Winston-Salem every weekend but one.

Fallbreak week, I lurked around bars frequented by Wake Forest University kids. I'd do one or two beers, then watch around me. Most girls wore make-up that made them look oh so young and far too old. I wasn't sure whether they'd done it on purpose or if it was something they didn't realize they'd done. Few looked happy or even as if they were enjoying themselves, though a lot of them carried themselves like they kind of thought they might be. It was weird, the way you could watch them down alcohol and see a sheen appear around them, as if they were staring at you from the other side of pieces of smoked glass, then they'd get all rubbery looking, head to toe. It was sad, the way they tried to keep big wet-looking smiles plastered across cosmetically enhanced features when they felt they were being watched. Until they got real rubbery. Then they didn't care any more. Or at least their bodies didn't.

When the bars closed, I'd drive home, sit in my room and eat a one-pound bag of Wise potato chips or half a box of Divinity cookies. During the days, I'd lie about the house, sleeping as late as I could make myself. When I woke, I'd read the *Norton Anthology of Oriental Masterpieces*, which I'd bought at the Wake Forest bookstore on my first day home. After gnawing at a few pages, I'd make myself sleep an hour or two more – storing up energy, I told myself.

When I couldn't stand bed or room or sleep any longer, I'd shuffle to the kitchen, pour a glass of iced tea and, even though my sister had sweetened the tea when she'd steeped it, I'd dump in a few more fat spoons of sugar. I'd lie on the sofa in the den, sip the golden sugar water and stare at reruns of *Get Smart* until Daddy came home from work and he and Carol fixed supper. Then I'd lock myself in my room, pop a James Brown 8-track into the player and begin a two-hour session of heavy-duty pimping up before hitting the bars.

I'm standing in front of the mirror in white cotton briefs. He's tall, at least seven-five. He's glaring down at me and His eyes are yellow. His face is a mass of old scar tissue. Maybe He was burned, I'm thinking. Then I see that His skin isn't white or black; it's grey. And He's not a man at all; His face is the only part made of flesh. From the shoulders down, He's a granite wall, literally. A wall that learned to walk, a wall shaped like a man.

We're going to fight, and I don't want to, but I sure ain't gonna let Him get off first. I zing Him with an eight-punch combination: straight-as-a-spear right lead to the heart; double right uppercut to His granite balls; triple hook – to the stone ribs, to the throat, one while leaping to His temple; another straight right, the punch thrown fast as a jab; a final sing-in-the-wind hook.

I raise my arms over my head, Ali-style, in victory. I thumb my nose at my fallen opponent like Bruce did in Enter the Dragon *and in* The Chinese Connection.

Twenty thousand fans in the Garden explode into applause.

Daddy steps into the room, *moving through the cheering throng, sidestepping New York's finest, hopping through the ropes.* He drops three pairs of clean black socks on my bed. 'Put these in your drawers, Dave,' he says.

II

OCTOBER, NOVEMBER, DECEMBER – researching, reading, thinking. Going for walks around the lake beside my dorm, where I watch the flapping of wings above water, and through boulder-encrusted woods, where I listen to the earth move, feeling it rotate inside me. I stop smoking stogies and drinking beer, almost without noticing I'd quit, having lost interest in S&M.

'Could I?' I regularly ask myself on those walks. 'Am I?' I quiz, studying the reflection in the bathroom mirrors. 'Will I?' I want to know, standing at the end of the hallway, peering out the window late at night.

By the first week of December I arrive at 'Where to start?'

12

WHERE HAD LEE begun? Maybe by leaving the University of Washington in his junior year, his interests apart from any major.

So were mine. I'd never get a degree in Lee and Ali studies or in limitless martial art. It was time to become serious (and playful): for Foetus to break out of the bag of waters. I couldn't see how I'd do that at Lose-McRae. Guys in the dorm, sitting around punching each other's arms, ragging on each other, laughing at each other's pain. Things they felt were important, I couldn't stand it. Pussy, food, dope, money, accounting; my dick's bigger'n yours. I mean, some of this stuff matters to me, too, but Lee had shown me another reality.

Their chief concerns seemed to include whether to order thin 'n' crispy or thick 'n' chewy pizzas, *I was weighing whether or not to commit my life to the ways (non-ways) of the warrior*, the present football season, *I would be the finest, most complete artist I could*, sliding down to the package store for a case of beer, *in the night, my skin would look wet with its light*, how and where to get some nookie on Saturday night, *the elegance of the elk would be mine*, where to buy answers to Mr Hall's Monday morning calculus exam, *as would the speed of the cheetah*, which girls would've looked better with bigger tits or smaller asses, *the grace of the impala, the deadliness of the black mamba*, and whether salaries were higher for those who'd majored in business or computer science. *And the explosiveness of a porpoise bursting into sky from out of the depths.*

No, I didn't see how I could stay a winter at Lose-McRae. The mountains were too damn cold already. I was tired of waking up to ice-covered trees and frozen roads. I'd had enough cold, enough winter, enough death.

I'd 'lived' death and witnessed a few of its faces. And had come to believe that there might be nothing in life but death, death itself being nothing, the nothing that keeps you from moving: *nichts, nada, niente, nihil, rien, sah mahng.*

Ali's was a vibrancy and rhythm only he could tap. Lee's was unusual, too, but he'd given indications of a life that could be mine. And I'd seen other intimations of life. In music, certainly, there *can* be life. There's death in music, too. That plaintive stuff you hear as fat-ass congregations of whitefolks sorrowfully, obligingly, sing of Christ bringing them alive. Maybe Jesus had something going (lots of people do). But Christ, how can any sane person take *anybody's followers* seriously? If taking them seriously ain't death, I don't know what is.

Yet I've heard, and felt, life in music. And I can't wait to listen, to investigate, further. I've felt life in dance, too: it's in the doing, in the moving with what is.

In writing? Yes, there's life in the act of writing. But one can appear to gain understanding through reading without knowing a damn thing. And reading many times brings sleep. Plus whatever you read is never as big as the experience it's about – and it's always in the past; it's dead. But writing is immediate: it's happening now: there's movement in writing, even if many writers are deathmongers. 'We are scabs and open wounds,' claims old dead Chaucer. Donkey poop. If we're scabs, we're scabs that *sing*! Or at least we try to.

Where else might I find life? In family? In home? I don't

know. So much of our notion of family life seems a well-intentioned, big-askew dream. Have you ever seen a family 'holiday celebration' where folks aren't aching and/or sleeping, just waiting for the damn turkey to get skeletonized so they can get the fuck out of Aunt Myrtle's and on with their lives? Well, maybe you have, I don't know, but this boy sure hasn't. It's almost all artifice. How can real celebration take place at appointed times, on appointed days? Too much form, too much robotics for me.

Can I find life through another person? A woman? What about love, that most prostituted of words? Can there be life in love? It can't be true when we say we've *fallen* in love; love is something you grow in. People who whine in pop songs about how they'd like to drown in a sea of love. I'd rather swim than sink. It may be possible to find life in love, but not in the Hallmark-card/pop-song-sappy way.

Yet. Right now. Right here. I know enough to begin.

Something, this thing that even when I was eleven years old a bit of me felt would happen, is happening, if I'll allow it. Why folks settle for something other than this something, I can't say. Children know that their parents are afraid to be alive. At least, I thought I knew it.

But, it doesn't matter. I'm certain that there can be life, and I'll be in it. I'll not settle for death, or for death posing as life.

Exams were coming up and that would be it, Lose-McRae would be gone, bye-bye, dead as history. I didn't know what I'd do for money (find a job; grow up, son), but I had to find out if I could fight, I had to write about martial art and Ali and Lee, and organized school was not the place to be. What I needed to know I'd not learn between the walls of any institution.

Lee had shown me that institutions were other façades behind which death lurked.

13

FOR THREE MONTHS I'd been poring through daily
newspapers in the library, hoping to spot a Lee movie
playing somewhere. This Thursday was the day. *Little
Dragon Lee Lives*, Baby Ruth style letters proclaimed.

Above this proclamation was a series of ideograms I
took to mean the same thing. Below, movie titles were
listed in the language I knew. Not one, but all three of
Lee's Hong Kong pictures: *The Big Boss*, *Fist of Fury* and
Way of the Dragon. It was a Bruce Lee festival! The name
of the cinema offering the tribute was the American, on
Bowery Street in New York's Chinatown. 'A special two-
week engagement – Starting Today!

'This may be your last chance to see Bruce's fast as
winds kick. His two legs sing quick as three in heroic
action. Also, Free Gift! A smart Bruce photo for you.'

The newspaper was six days old. I hurried to the room
and packed a change of clothes. $114.17 in the bank. The
remainder of my allowance for the semester. In Boone I
filled the Camaro with 24.9 cents per gallon premium,
ran it through a car wash and was on my way, off and
ready to take a chomp out of the Huge Ole Apple.

I drove straight through the night, stopping to fuel-up,
chow-down, piss and stretch. I tooled the Camaro into
Manhattan through the Lincoln Tunnel. It was Friday
morning at eight. I saw more people in half an hour than
I'd seen in my whole life. Frozen in traffic, I watched a
sad-looking woman in her forties walk up the street in an

expensive purple dress and coat, high-heeled purple shoes and purple beehive hairstyle, walking her purple poodle on a purple rhinestone-studded leash. Two police cars played bumper tag at fifteen miles per hour. The chrome and steel made crunching noises, the policemen's heads were tossed sharply forwards, they creaked the cars apart, threw their heads back in open-mouthed, drunken laughter – then they conjugated the automobiles again and laughed some more. I had no reason to believe they'd been drinking.

I saw cabbies scream yellow *watchoutI'mcoming!* vehicles through red lights at somewhere near fifty miles an hour, without apparently looking in either direction, finding openings where there seemed to be none. I watched another policeman's billy stick thump a passed-out man on the head in front of Madison Square Garden. I saw a man in an eighth-floor window shoot a BB rifle at passers-by while yet another policeman watched and shook his head and laughed. I watched a nattily-dressed old man shuffle up the street with an empty grocery bag all the way down over his head. Then I drove back to New Jersey, where I took a room at a Howard Johnson's.

Mid-afternoon, I glided into the dank dark world of a packed Chinatown cinema. *Where have all these people come from at this time of day?* The crowd was screaming, clapping, laughing. I sat as still as I could and studied the full Bruce Lee saga. Only one of the movies was subtitled. All three were in Chinese. I couldn't understand a word, but felt I got what Lee was saying, anyway.

After the third and best movie, *Way of the Dragon*, I left Chinatown and New York and drove straight to the Howard Johnson's, where I slept a couple hours, too fired up to stay in bed, grabbed wholewheat toast and juice – no more doughnuts and sodas for this kid! – and started down I-95 to bigger better beautiful Banner Elk, having seen the sights I wanted to see.

14

I'M NOT AFRAID of them. Not any more. They've hurt old people and children and women and animals and the world and wimps and themselves. I'll not be hurt again.

Ignorance lies heavy on their tongues. Films of sleep cloud their eyes. Arfmann and King Mobeley; Romo and Weso, too. I stand before them. My body glows ripe with the rainbow hovering around me, the rainbow my fear creates.

And they come. I feel yellow and orange break from one end of the spectrum and spring as beams from my fingertips. Vermilion jets ease quickly off my toes. And they bow: Romo and Arfmann and Sam Stone. They fall: Richard J. Reynolds and Tom Buchanan and careless ole shithead Daisy. Where they bow, there they fall and they look up to me. Their eyes have come alive. I reach to them, help them to their feet. They smile and understand. So do I. And I wake, happy.

It was an unusually warm afternoon for December. High in the mid-fifties. I walked from Avery Dorm over to Wildcat Lake, watched and listened to waves lap non-music against the shore.

I kicked off shoes, socks, felt ground beneath my feet. God, it felt good.

Hell, yes, I'd do it.

I'd get clean and dirty. The two aren't separate. I'd bathe in dreams and in lightning.

Images of fresh green and yellow vegetables, crisp red and orange fruits, and a life beyond cynicism flashed behind my eyes. I tried to imagine what it'd be like to catch a sanctified buzz off a tall cold glass of water.

I closed my eyes, took my first real breath of real air in years. Opened them, took another slow one, and smiled. I was going to do good stuff; more than that, I'd *be* good stuff.

Packed books and clothes, pulled the Ali poster and Lee pictures from the wall and left a handwritten copy of a Zen koan on the mattress, the one I'd read in my religions of the world book, about how to remove a live goose from a thin-necked bottle without harming the bird or the container:

There, it's out!

Loaded the trunk and back seat of the Camaro, filled up with gas, slid Stevie Wonder's *Inner Visions* into the tape deck, and tooled towards home. Exams? What exams? Late-afternoon sun felt fine filtering through tinted windows. I was as awake as a pen-kept dog about to be set loose in the woods. Halfway to Boone, I rolled down the window and smilingly tossed my Ben Hogan up and out into the emptiness.

Made a stop at a sporting goods store in Boone. Trotting towards the Camaro in the first sweatsuit and running shoes I'd owned – and minus the remainder of my Lose-McRae allowance – I felt great. My life had begun.

PART TWO

A NEW LIFE

Is not the flute that soothes
the very one that was cut from wood with knives?

Kahlil Gibran

15

I'M IN DR BUTLER'S office, my father's doc who looks like that asshole Jesse Helms. Despite this liability, Dr Butler's a nice guy. My whole life, I've seen Dr B. when I've been out and around with Daddy, but I've never been to him as a patient. I've always visited my paediatrician, Dr Glenn. At almost twenty-two, this is my first visit to a grown-up's doc.

Dr Butler pokes, prods and thumps on me here, there and most everywhere, then gives his OK to begin training. 'But', he says, wagging his finger at me, 'you'd better start light.'

I laugh out loud. Not at Dr Butler – but at me. My puny little body would implode on the spot if I even dreamed of starting 'heavy'.

Tugging down my T-shirt after Dr B has listened to my heart, I ask if the big chocolate-coloured birthmark on the right side of my chest means anything.

'I reckon it's something you'll have to live with, son,' he says, chuckling. Then, 'It's nothing to worry about,' he assures me. 'Here's something interesting on the X-ray, though. Did you know you have an extra rib?' He pats what I hope will become my well-packed right pectoral muscles. 'Right about here – under all that excess pigment.'

He laughs again and turns towards the door. 'Guess that means there's no woman for you.'

It's a joke I don't understand. Looking over his

shoulder, he sees I'm puzzled. 'Don't you read your Bible, son? – Woman was created from one of man's ribs.'

I laugh out of politeness, but later at home, looking at my chest in the mirror, I begin to worry about the awful possibility. No woman for me.

Standing in the bathroom late at night, staring in the mirror once again. Well, what d'ya know? Funny I've never noticed. The birthmark on my chest *is* the same shape as that of mainland China.

16

I START MY Lee-inspired workouts in the second week of January 1974, just before my birthday. On Daddy's bathroom scales I weigh in at ninety-two pounds. Push though I may (and I do), I'm unable to perform a single push-up. I try them stooped on all-fours, what we called 'women's' push-ups in high school gym class.

When I've worn myself out on a (very) few of these, I run twice around Daddy's half-acre backyard, my legs stiff, tripping in mole holes and almost falling. I finish my day with ten overhead presses with the twenty-two-pound, baby-blue, plastic weight set Daddy'd tried to motivate me with when he'd bought it for me the year after my mother had died. The next morning I'm so sore I can hardly lift my arms over my head.

All through the winter and spring I stay with my workouts, and soon I'm able to run five times round the yard – then ten, fifteen, twenty. I dig deep every day and after a few months I sprint the last five laps and bound down the creek bank, through the water and up the other side and I churn through the woods and briars, then follow the creek all the way down to Shaffner Park and back, creating my own ambling four-mile path.

By then I'm squeezing out push-ups in multiples: three sets of ten, twenty, then thirty-five, now fifty; eventually, I get up to grinding out more than five hundred a day.

In January I started with five sit-ups per workout; one year later, I'm at one thousand, six days a week, every single week. And a couple hundred crunches and leg raises on top of that. Like Lee, I teach myself to do push-ups on my fingertips; and on the thumb and forefinger of each hand; and even, eventually, to perform one-arm push-ups.

Eating four overflowing multi-plate meals every sixteen hours, then adding a gallon of whole milk and a couple blenders of ground-up ice cream, bananas and Bob Hoffman's quick weight-gain powder, I force the bathroom scales to 105 then 112, 119, 121.

I remember walking past the mirror in just a pair of gym shorts and spotting a muscular torso out of the corner of my left eye: crisply defined pecs, trapezius, lats, deltoids, everything. For part of a second, I wonder who this person is in the mirror. Then I smile . . . though I'm still not sure this is *my* image.

I order a blue-vinyl punching bag from an advertisement in a karate magazine, and when it comes, I pack it with rags and a couple worn-out pillows. I shove fists and feet into its man-made hide day after day, night after night. After several months I purchase an Everlast pre-packed ninety-pound black leather bag from Bocock-Stroud's Sporting Supplies and empty the stuffings from my blue-vinyl critter into the garbage can, refilling its flattened husk with more than a hundred pounds of sand from the creek behind Daddy's.

For my twenty-second birthday, Daddy'd bought me a wooden-handled, damn fine leather jump-rope. I'd watched Ali work with ropes and there was an instruction booklet attached to one of the handles. At first I step on the rope and trip over it and hurt my ankles and shins and calves and almost fall with every turn. I bend my knees too, instead of holding them straight, and use my arms when I should turn it only with my wrists. But I'm not embarrassed not to know what I'm doing. In fact, I'm surprised I'm not self-conscious about anything much I'm trying, even if it is amazing how quick the rope gets me tired and I find myself gasping and wheezing like an emphysema victim.

But I sure do get good with that thang. The day comes when I can tap into a big bunch of different rhythms and scramble them all up in any order I want: jump with a skipping stutter-step one leg at a time; move laterally across the floor; backwards and forwards, up and down the floor; whip the rope beneath my feet two turns for every time I jump; even jump while hobbling around in a full squat, looking like some huge crustacean.

I become entranced by the wondrously soothing and stimulating sounds of my rope slapping concrete and of a well-worked speedbag bouncing back and forth on its wooden platform. I hang an Everlast 4204 Turbo over in the corner and commune with the small bag's shining leather bladder for close to half an hour per workout.

And, by my standards, I'm becoming A BIG, STRONG, HUMONGOUS, GIANT SUMGUN. Within a couple years I'm up to ten consecutive three-minute rounds on the rope and on each of three heavy bags – the Everlast for punches, kicks, knees and elbows; the one filled with sand for open-hand blows; the third and lightest one for high kicks.

Day after day, month after month, I go down to the basement to dance with my Everlast. It's always there, hanging sure and straight and silent in the centre of the room, seeming to fill most of the 1,500-square-foot space. I rip into the bag with hands and feet, concentrating on speed – godly speed, quickly discovering that the more relaxed I am, the faster, more powerful and more precise techniques become. Eventually I get to where I can zing four, six, even eight shots per second. By this time, I recognize I'm maybe the second or third fastest human I've ever seen.

As I work the Everlast, I sometimes finish rounds with

a step-across side-kick. When I pump the side-kick well, it bends the big bag nearly in two and swings it up and away, towards thick cedar beams creaking in the ceiling. At the top of its flight it seems to hang and, just when there's cause to wonder if Newton's Law has been suspended, it starts to fall – a steam-driven piston that lands with a bright concussive *Claung!* and a jerk that shakes dust and splinters from the rafters and plaster from the walls.

I become enraptured not only with the heft of the Everlast and its reliability, but with the feel of sweat on my skin. I get to where I can't stand to wear unnecessary clothes – and come to think of most shirts and trousers as just that: not needed.

The judge does not agree. During my second summer of training, I receive a traffic citation for driving without having my licence with me. (I'd stopped carrying a wallet, not wanting to be burdened with it; it limited my freedom of movement.) As the ticket is being written, I'm told by the arresting officer that if I bring my licence to court, the charges will probably be dropped. On the appointed morning, I go for an early run, then tool down to the courthouse with my licence – barefoot, shirtless, wearing a pair of workout shorts. As the flat-top sporting judge enters the chambers, he spies me, seated in the gallery. He points and frowns, then waves me forward. I rise calmly from my seat and amble over to the well-polished mahogany guardrail, glowingly confident of my own rightness. 'I'll give you twenty minutes to find yourself some clothes,' he says, short and hard. For the life of me, I don't understand why he's upset. But I leave, to return wearing T-shirt and shoes.

First thing each morning and fifteen minutes before bed every night, I perform upper and lower body stretches. I find a short, square, Japanese-style table in an import shop, which I buy, along with a green clay garden Buddha. I place the Buddha at the rear of the table, an incense burner in its lap, and line up five small candles near the front of the table. Every night, after my evening stretches, I light the candles, turn off the electric lights, and sit naked before the Buddha, meditating while listening to my Marvellous Marvin Gaye record, *Let's Get It On*. On the way to bed, I snuff out all five candles with a series of air-popping kicks and punches.

I move towards sleep, rock myself to sleep, am asleep. Marvin Gaye's voice continues to fill the room.

Music is real. High notes rise in the air, low ones burrow into the earth. The world becomes the sound.

I stand. At the edge of a forest. Seeing the green of leaves, light and dark of birch bark, watching the way the breeze moves branches and trunks, feeling the breeze on my skin.

I study effects of the wind, listen to songs of the wind, feel the wind make my skin sing. I become the wind. I know its melodies, hum its songs. No one need tell me where to stand.

I buy a full-length mirror which I place against a wall in the basement and spend an hour a day shadow-boxing in front of it; half an hour of free-form punching: jab, jab, jabjabjab, back-fist, more jabs, different style jabs, switch sides and jab with the right, different back-fists, left hooks, a whipping motion on the end of some jabs to approximate the power of a hook, overhand rights, right leads; then a second half-hour making the air snap and pop with kick combinations – front-kick, side-kick; round-kick, hook-kick, side-kick; crescent-kick, spinning reverse crescent-kick, round-kick. All of it feels so fine and liberating that I actually begin to wonder if I might not be able to teach myself to fly.

After thirty minutes of punching and another thirty of kicks, I combine kicks, punches and hand strikes for a few rounds. As I throw techniques, I suck air in deep and blow it out hard, giving myself, in effect, a continual series of Zen slaps, seeking to constantly wake myself. Popping the air with blows too fast to count, I imagine lightning coursing through my limbs. Always patterning my style on what I've seen Lee do in the movies and on Ali's boxing (as well as on what feels glowingly natural), I find rhythms and a suppleness I feel have been asleep inside me. My Lee-inspired workouts also help me feel, for the first time ever, that I'm not a fraud – that, indeed, I'm one very real slice.

And, as I'll discover years later, as is true of the very best sex, (many) moments occur in which you know you're not the one doing the moving, but that you're living inside the movement. And I learn something else fundamental: there ain't nothin' a human being can do, no matter how impossible it may at first seem, that another one can't do, too.

Someone's standing in front of me. He's naked. His lean golden torso refracts light, breaks it gently and it wavers near him in prisms. At first I don't know this man. Then I see that he's me. Only I'm unashamed of my nakedness. And my face has sprouted a thick glowing beard I know, even in the dream, that I can't grow. I'm playing a flute. Not with mouth or hands. The pipe is part of my body. The instrument plays itself.

I apply for a job at the convenience store where I used to buy beer and I know the manager on a first-name basis. Jim hires me to work second shift, which allows me to support my martial addiction – not only by giving me a few dollars – but also because, when I'm in the store by myself, I read all the martial arts and boxing rags on the magazine rack. Between customers, I do push-ups, stretch, a little shadow; think up, work on and polish combinations until they gleam. It's the first job I've had. I'm surprised how much I enjoy it.

I recall getting in from work one 1974 midnight and spooning out a few vegetables Daddy's left simmering on the stove, carrying my plate into the den. While I stand with the plate in my right hand, forking stewed carrots into my mouth with the left, watching Johnny Carson while standing barefoot on the carpet, I throw three – count 'em, THREE! – whippingly wonderful and beatifically beautiful round-kicks, all without touching my foot to the floor, cleanly snapping the heads from all three porcelain Cupid statuettes, who are sitting there minding their own business on a bookshelf high up over to the left side of the TV.

I'm not upset by this (after all, consider the control it took to perform this beauteous feat); rather, I'm amazed – 'Hey, wow, cool,' I must've said – then, when I finish my final meal of the day and reach some level of post-martial sobriety, I try to repair my dead mom's old figurines with Elmer's wood glue.

When I'm not working out or pulling time at the convenience store, I'm studying Lee and Ali, sometimes in cinemas, sometimes on TV and, most often, in free movies that roll behind my eyes. And I'm devouring all the Lee/Ali magazines – as well as every book and periodical about martial art and boxing – that I can find. My interest in real writing, in literary storytelling, keeps growing. I reread the novels from Karen's class at Lees-McRae and ask clerks in bookstores what fiction they enjoy most. I find more and more good writers that way. And the world gets bigger and bigger.

And then. I'm at 123, and 26, 28, 31, 35 and 140 (the same weight Lee had been most of his adult years). What keeps me fascinated with martial art, day in and day out, is the belief that I'm doing something – shine on, shine on

– and even more powerful, I have the sense that in every moment there's something extraordinary to learn, some lush place that is throbbingly, achingly remarkable to go.

I'm alone in a small, mirrored room, sitting in the middle of the wooden floor, relaxing and listening to my body hum as it cools. I slowly stand, step to the mirrors and leap into a jumping spinning crescent-kick. When I should plop to the floor, I keep levitating up. I cross my legs, close my eyes, sit on the air and float. I know entirely, exactly what I am doing; I am in absolute control. I sense someone at the door and glide to the floor, remaining in a full lotus. One of my students enters the room and asks if I've been training.

'I've just finished,' I say, and then I wake, happy and laughing, full of my body-buzz, filled with the power of the dream, full of belief in the dream, and with the knowledge that, yes, I can do it – I can fly.

I practise hundreds of techniques and skills, including jabs, straight rights, overhand rights, hooks, uppercuts, back-fists, spinning back-fists, hammer-fists, a bushel basket of eye jabs and gouges, open-palm strikes; arm and wrist locks, elbows, head-butts, knees; front-kicks, round-kicks, side-kicks snapped to the head, dug into the abdomen, thrust through the knees; back-kicks, spinning back-kicks, crescent-kicks, hook-kicks, shin-kicks; a plethora of stomps, jumps, spins, feints, fakes, draws, counters, blocks; immobilization tactics, in-and-out and side-to-side movement, defensive head movement, et cetera, et cetera, et cetera: I learn lots about the human body, the ways it moves and the precise co-ordination of these moves required to tell a good martial story. And I'm proud of who I'm becoming. There's no way Lee himself could've worked more diligently; I push myself hard nearly every waking hour.

Occasionally, I even manage to use my newly honed skills to punch and kick people. And get punched and kicked in return. Once or twice I attempt to do so against some capable and wilful folks.

17

IT'S A BRIGHT, cold, windy morning in April 1976. Tuesday, my day off from the store. I'm running five miles on the path behind Daddy's house. Sunlight flashes through tender green shoots that have sprung from overhanging branches of willows. I don't feel the cold on my skin, only in my lungs, where it burns as it rushes in with each breath: two steps – breathe in through nose and mouth; two more – out with a whoosh, unbelievably grateful to be able to release warm, wet steam clouds back into the day, feeling the thawing loam under my Pumas.

Dallas is running with me and he's a welcome partner. After all, he's the only guy I know who doesn't think I'm nuts for running not only forwards, but backwards, sideways and cross-legged, skipping, leaping into forward rolls and tossing jabs, hooks and uppercuts at tree limbs and launching round-kicks and flying side-kicks at every telephone pole we pass.

But some folks think Dallas isn't normal, either. Hell, Dallas doesn't even look like your average pooch. In some ways, he more resembles a cow than a canine. His daddy was Dalmatian, his mama English bull and, since he's the one puppy in his litter that lived, that makes him, to the best of my knowledge, the world's first and only bullmatian. He has a Dalmatian's long legs, speed, spots, playfulness and stinky-ass skin; and he inherited his mama's good looks – the squashed Joe Frazier face (and fighting skill), a twenty-five-inch neck and Arnold Schwarzenegger shoulders and chest. Some people think Dallas is ugly. I think Dallas is almost as pretty as me.

As we push through the wind and bound past the house, Daddy steps out of the back door to leave for work. He yells, 'Look out for your sister, Dave.' I wave and shift concentration back to my run, losing myself to my body's sweet, warm songs.

That evening, when Daddy gets in from work, I've just picked myself up from the cocoon-like impression I've made in the carpet in front of the TV, after completing a few hundreds sits and pushes. My back is turned to the door and I'm in the furthest corner of the den, slinging combinations at squat-bodied samurais as they erupt up from under the floors, jump down from the ceiling, spring out from behind walls. The wind makes the windows howl and squeak and moan. I bob and weave under a waist-wide sword being swung by a short, fast, hard little man, slide to the right, front-kick up through his intra-articular fat pad into the backside of his left knee. He drops his weapon as he's slammed against the wall.

I feel Daddy behind me before he says, 'Hello, son.'

I turn to greet him, glad he's home early. But I'm at the height of my shadow-fighting fantasy; I'm pumped up bigtime. I wheel towards him and smile, big and loose. 'Pops,' I say, 'check this out.'

I jet a couple quick shots towards his face, maybe a quarter of an inch away, just playing in a serious way, having fun.

'Stop, son,' he says, startled, backing up.

'Relax,' I say, chuckling at his insecurity, not seeing how tired he is. 'I ain't gonna hit you.'

He leans towards me a little. The next technique I throw catches him flush on his left cheek, under the eye. It's a close-fisted shot that explodes into his face. His head is snapped back and to the left. Unlike the guys Lee pounds on in the movies, Daddy's face doesn't go bright with the thrill of pain. As the colour flows from his cheeks, he looks sick and very old. Utterly reduced.

My father bites down hard on his lower lip, turns and walks to his room, closing the door. I don't know what to say or do. For minutes and minutes, I stand right where I am, on almost exactly the spot where I punched him.

After a long while I work up the nerve to knock on his door; he doesn't answer.

Daddy never says a word to me about hitting him. And I don't say anything to him. But I'm never that careless with my tools again.

Over the next few weeks, the swelling under Daddy's eye washes away from purple and brown to yellow, then disappears. But the bruise is still there. Both in him and in me.

18

IF PUNCHING MY dad in the eye is one of the worst things that happened because of my years of living life at the end of fists, here are some of the best:

1

I've driven to Greenville, North Carolina to visit my friend Tony Lopez. We're showing his students how to cut-off the ring, a skill useful to competitive fighters and to folks accosted in alleys.

I have hands up beside my head and chin tucked in next to my shoulder. With forearms, then palms, Tony shoves me into a corner and shows how to wondrously dig palms and fists into biceps to bring hands down, when to beautifully shovel fingers and elbows into spaces between ribs near the heart, how to majestically thrust knees, shins and feet into kidneys/groin/bladder. In this otherwise ordinary moment, I recognize the arc of my life.

Through Tony's appendages, I'm part of a big family. Our kin includes every person who has had ten-ounce sheaths of cows' hide grow on to the ends of his arms. It includes everyone who has felt music in the hypnotically repetitive *futada-futada* sound of a properly worked speed bag and who understands the relationship between this call and a rhythm inside himself.

World superlightweight kick-boxing champion Tony

'Huracan' Lopez is the most well-rounded martial artist I've known – one of the best fighters, weapons and forms competitors in the world, and the only guy who has ever been world ranked in each of these categories. Good enough to have kicked around Jhoon Rhee, with whom he studied. Rhee, credited with bringing tae kwon do to America and one of Bruce Lee's best friends, took from and gave to Li Siu Loong himself. Lee studied under Yip Man, 'The Gentle Whirlwind', who escaped from mainland China in 1949 and carried to Hong Kong the gung fu style called *wing chun*. From Shaolin nun Yim Wing Chun, 'The Daughter of Beautiful Springtime', to monks in her monastery, to old Bodhidharma, the Indian sage reputed to have brought Buddhism and the fighting arts to China, I'm related to them all.

Our relationship is kinetic. Bruce Lee and Tony Lopez and I. Probably even old Bodhidharma.

Warriors and healers, monks and lovers, creatures of intellect and of flesh and of spirit. We are hard and soft, fast yet careful, strong yet graceful. Snow clouds, fog, wind, thunder, blue skies in February and in August, drizzle, monsoons, hurricanes; there is power and beauty in all weather.

2

Early Saturday morning. I'm on my way back to Daddy's from a run up to Reynolda Gardens, where Silas Creek begins. Walking home beside the creek, I watch insects as they crawl through grass, waves created by the wind on a puddle, a mockingbird as it springs from tree to tree – singing a different song on every branch, the colour of a pretty girl's shoes, doors as they open and close behind me. The waters are calm; I'm the moon on the stream. *Nagare Sausa.*

3

My face has sprouted a thick glowing beard I know I can't grow. I'm playing a flute. Not with mouth or hands. The pipe is part of my body. The instrument plays itself.

Behind me, in a mirror, stands a woman. She's young and strong. Bushels of long, loose curls spill from her shoulders. Her scent rises bright in the air. It's the fragrance of waterfalls and wind and the skin of peaches. She's admiring the music and its instrument.

She reads from a small, worn leather book. She says: 'Is not the flute that soothes, the very one carved from wood with knives?'

Early summer 1976: a year of the dragon. I've felt for more than two years that this is when *this* has to happen.

The morning train rumbles by, its whistle moaning as the sound drifts in my window from over off Stratford Road. I lie in bed a few minutes and gaze at leaves on sugar maples in the backyard, and ones on the water oaks, and on the river birches, and the willows and weeping cherries, and at all the fescue sprouting in all the yards.

I stand, pull on a pair of white gym shorts and ease into a few slow stretches, first palming the floor, then touching nose and chin to knees. I hobble to the kitchen, pop a couple slices of wheat bread in the toaster, open the refrigerator and syphon a giant gulp of skimmed milk straight from the carton, then walk out to the front yard and draw a few deep breaths of air.

I watch the mailman make his rounds, the business guys all sad and empty-eyed on their way to the nine to fives, turn and stare at my earthen path, which follows the creek as it lopes lazily behind Daddy's house, smile and think, 'Man, I'm one lucky son of a gun.'

About noon, I lace up an old pair of Adidas, open the

back door and sprint across the yard and down to the creek, sail up the bank on the other side and on to my path. Smelly ole Dallas falls in beside me. 'Hey, woofa,' I say, and bend to greet him with a tug on his flopping jowls.

I kick my legs high, churning stones and last year's leaves beneath my feet, take air in through mouth and nose, and blow it out in short, hot *fuuhs*. As we start up the short incline that leads to Shaffner, Dallas thunders ahead, his feet splashing waves of dust behind him. As I top the hill, I see him chasing two setters, one Irish, one English, through the field below.

At a dead run, I pump out the last two hundred yards between the dogs and me. As I run, I whip Dallas's leash from where I've been keeping it tied round my waist and, as I pull up beside him, I slap it on his collar. He realizes I've chained him, digs his claws into the turf, and heaves forward with his shoulders, dragging me a few feet before I yank him up short beside me.

'Davis, hey, where'd you get that big, weird mutt?' a girl's voice calls from between laughs behind me. I turn to find Emily Crews, a cute sixteen-year-old who's a customer at the convenience store – she regularly comes in to flirt and buy sodas – standing a few feet away.

I explain that Dallas is no mutt; he's a full-blooded bullmatian, but she keeps on laughing. 'Lyn,' she calls over her shoulder, 'you've got to see this dog. Davis says he's some kind of "damnation". Doesn't he look like Petey on *The Little Rascals*?'

A girl appears from behind a slab of limestone down by the creek. She's barefoot and wearing a pair of cut-offs and a skimpy white tank-top. And she's braless. She has big brown animal eyes and almost waist-length curly auburn hair that's thick as a horse's main. I've seen this girl before. We talked a little at the party after my third pro fight.

She steps over and Emily introduces us. 'Davis Miller, this is my friend Lyn Spencer.'

Lyn smiles. My legs go weak and numb and my mouth feels that it may not work when I try to open it. 'Davis,' she says in a way I've never heard my name pronounced. 'Davis Miller,' she repeats, as if the words mean something. 'You have a nice tan,' she says.

I don't tell her that I don't have time to lie in the sun. 'Thanks,' I say, struggling to get out the words. 'So do you.'

On our first date, Lyn and I take in a movie. We go to see – what else? – *Enter the Dragon*, which has been re-released and is playing downtown at the Carolina Theatre. The 1976 National AAU Boxing Championships are taking place in Winston-Salem this same weekend. Ray Leonard, Howard Davis, Michael and Leon Spinks, and other pugilists sit in the row behind us during the movie.

At the end several boxers ask for a ride to their hotel. Lyn and I squeeze room for five of them in the Camaro, four in back, one up front. Lyn has to slide right up next to me (like I mind), one leg on each bucket seat and the gear stick between her thighs. We drive across town to the Ramada Inn near the airport. On the way we all talk about Lee. 'Little man hits hard,' I remember one boxer saying. 'Looks like he hits hard as a heavyweight.'

As we drop off the fighters, Lyn asks if I'll buy her a beer. We stop by the store and pick up a couple eight-ounce bottles of Miller, then drive to Shaffner Park. Almost as soon as I slip the gear stick into neutral and switch off the lights, I feel compelled to show Lyn some of my very best stuff.

I get out of the car, kick off my sandals in the grass, do side stretches by placing one foot then the other atop the roof, then dance around the Camaro, zinging punches and kicks as quick and juicy as I ever have in my life, so fired up to be with her and finally have somebody to share *Enter the Dragon* with – not to mention loosened up by the first beer I've drunk in three years – that I do something I've never even thought about trying in front of anyone: I emulate Lee's tomcat-eating-a-chicken *kiaii*.

'*Waa-saa!*' I screech and look at Lyn for a reaction. She doesn't laugh at me. Her eyes are open saucer-wide and she's smiling. I think she's impressed.

At first: it's organs and blood, muscle and bones and connective tissue. There's the groping.

Then: 'Trust me,' you say. And you touch my hips, guiding me, yet allowing me to guide myself. Then that part of me that enters you becomes me, in that moment. Then there's not even that. No me, no you. Nothing to prove, nowhere to be, nothing larger to do.

4

'I am all styles yet I am no style,' said Bruce Lee.

How and why did I come from martial art to make a life struggling to sculpt elegant sentences and paragraphs? Three reasons worth mentioning: throw five thousand exacting punches and kicks per day for several years and the idea of rewrites isn't terribly imposing; after you've been hit in the face with a few qualified fists and feet, a couple of humbling reviews ain't the most frightening of possibilities; and internalizing the intensity I found radiating from Lee allowed me to access the rigorous, beautiful, primeval writing place inside me.

Yet the very thing that gave me the courage to write is that through my experiences in martial arts I'd learned not to take what I did, or didn't do, personally. As I wasn't performing martial art, but was a vessel through which the art poured, so I would be a vehicle through which words flowed.

Oh, and one more thing. When I stumbled upon Lee in *Enter the Dragon*, for the first time in my life, suddenly I was awake. Today, I still see with fresh eyes. I don't know of a quality more important (or more grandly discomforting) for someone who feels he needs to write.

All through the mid-1970s, until I met Lyn, Lee and his movies had been both my fever and the cure, the dream and the life. During that time, between rocketing tens of millions of kicks and hand strikes, I'd watched *Enter the Dragon* and Lee's three other films dozens of times. Again and again, off I'd go, to my personal haven of fairy-tale violence, to the fabled land of Fistiana, that place where the plastic scars always stick and pigs' blood ceaselessly flows.

In 1973 and 1974 Lee movies had been shown in middle-class shopping malls and uptown cinemas, but by 1975, in search of enlightenment, I'd descend into dark, cool confines of inner-city cinemas, the air reeking of urine and Thunderbird wine. I'd take my seat among a couple of dozen screaming black folks, a few aspiring white street toughs, and occasionally a drunk old man who'd wake from his catatonia, jump from his seat, and scream, 'Kill that muhfucka', whenever characters stopped talking and Lee hit someone.

All these years later, I reveal so much of my story not in self-revelation and mostly not for ego gratification, but because I believe it says much about Lee's screen image, the dream he developed, and the innate, supremely powerful effect he had – and continues to have – on his core audience: the lonely, the frustrated, the inarticulate, the disaffected, the downtrodden, the half-asleep.

And, in particular, on those who believe that, when they first see Lee, they are irrevocably liberated from that stupor.

PART THREE

A LITTLE HISTORY

Everything dies
Baby that's a fact
Maybe everything that dies
Someday comes back.

Bruce Springsteen

19

FACE AS FACELESS as God: few people have attained this, the ultimate, ethicless, unqualified fame. Among names which come to mind: Jesus, Buddha, Muhammad.

Perhaps only four people from the twentieth century can be considered for this list:

1 Adolf Hitler
2 Muhammad Ali (always Ali)
3 Elvis Presley

and, yes, surprisingly,

4 Bruce Lee.

Vague visions of midnight street wars, lost powers, hidden rhythms, secret techniques: Vibrating Butterfly Palms, Delayed Death Touches, Sleeping Hands, Whirling Dragon Tails, swirl like exploding Chinese skyrockets seen through a mist.

Actor James Coburn has said, 'Bruce was more dynamic than anyone else I've met. He could go from zero to one-forty in no time at all – *pow!* and he'd be gone.'

Movie director Blake Edwards has conjectured that the problem in his relationship with Lee 'was that there was never a moment I wasn't in awe of him'.

Academy Award-winning screenwriter Stirling Siliphant confided, 'All my life I've known only idiots. I define an idiot as a person who makes himself less than he could be by blaming his actions on something, or someone, outside himself. The only non-idiot I've known, the only person I've seen who exercised his abilities, whether physical or intellectual, to the highest possible degree, is Bruce Lee.'

Those who don't practise martial art regard Lee's movies almost as respectfully as Three Stooges shorts – Larry bonks Moe on his noggin, Moe sticks his fingers in Larry's eyes, Larry stomps on Curly's foot – but there are others who take Bruce Lee very seriously. Three decades after his death, Lee is revered by martial arts practitioners throughout the world; his likeness is sold in boutiques in Beverly Hills and in souks in Marrakesh, hangs on apartment walls in Kiev and in Paris, in mud huts in central African nations and in the Australian outback, as well as on the insides of gym lockers in Peoria and Liverpool; his image is the one that's still most common on the cover of martial arts publications world-round; his ambiguous reputation as the twentieth-century god of martial art is known in almost every city, town, and village on the planet.

Though relatively few of us have seen Lee or one of his few movies, his name may be recognized in more places than that of anyone else of our time. Jhoon Rhee, American tae kwon do legend, tells of a 1992 trip to Russia. 'When I was shopping in Moscow, everywhere there were Bruce Lee posters and Muhammad Ali posters. I asked a lot of people, "Who is most famous, Muhammad Ali or Bruce Lee?" I was so surprised to hear, unanimously, "Bruce Lee".'

Within two years of Lee's death, his name had become a cliché. Bruce Lee; a pseudonym to be tagged on to every side-kicker in every *dojo*, arena, *dojang*, gym, *kwoon*, movie-studio lot, or back alley.

Consider those Hong Kong movies of the mid-1970s, the ones that thoroughly diminished Lee's story and had titles such as *Bruce Lee Strikes Back from the Grave*, *The Clones of Bruce Lee* and *Bruce Lee Goes to Hell*, and which starred a legion of grimacing and screeching, pseudo-similar androids such as Bruce Li, Bruce Le, Bruce Lei, Bruce Lo, Myron Bruce Lee, (Charles) Bronson Lee, Dragon Lee, Bruce Tease, Bruce Sleaze, Bruce Quease, Spruce Trees, Loose Leaves.

A fog of rumour, myth and mystery continues to surround the circumstances of Lee's death. Among the most popular theories: he died from overtraining or from too much sex; he was murdered by angry kung fu masters; by the Chinese 'Mafia'; he was poisoned by an evil herbalist; killed by a secret society of martial arts assassins; by the director of his first two movies (fewer than three weeks before his death, Lee had threatened this director – who'd been goading him for weeks – with a knife hidden in his belt buckle); by the head of the movie studio for which he worked, who, through the remainder of the century, would reap hundreds of millions of dollars from Lee's legend; by rival Hong Kong movie magnates, who were rumoured to be jealous of, and infuriated by, Lee's success; by Lee's lover(s); by his wife; by big mythological dragons angered that he had called himself Small Dragon Lee. Or that he had an unsuspected congenital condition that became lethal because of the intensity with which he lived. And maybe most fabulously, that Lee had not died, but had gone into seclusion, in the Shaolin temple/a cave in the jungles of south-east Asia/a remote mountaintop. And that he'd return at some date – *the turn of the millennium*? 2000 is the next year of the dragon. And Lee's sixtieth birthday.

To me, man-nova Bruce Lee's *real* life is more intriguing than these quasi-religious myths. Lee was a flawed, complex, yet singular talent whose reputation, in death, has been even more abused than Elvis's – Presley basics have been correctly reported hundreds of times. Yet, despite Lee's world-wide fame and his effect on global culture, no one has written about him truthfully or well. Indeed, if Ali is the most famous fellow of the twentieth century whom we know most about, Lee is the one about whom we know least. Celluloid and print fictions have dramatically marginalized him and his impact on society. Few of us have a clue what Lee said, felt, dreamed, did, or didn't do. The mist of money-making myth around him is so thick that the truth of his story has been almost entirely obscured. It's time some of this fog got burned away.

The reality is this: in the three years immediately preceding his death Bruce Lee revolutionized the martial arts and for ever changed action movie-making. He became the first truly international film luminary (popular not only in the United States, Great Britain and Europe, but in Asia, the Soviet Union, the Middle East and on the Indian subcontinent – in those pre-Spielberg days people in most nations were not particularly worshipful of the Hollywood hegemony). Until now Lee has received little credit for these accomplishments.

Think of Gatsby and his optimistic, orderly, yet doomed pursuit of the dream. An important literary figure begins to emerge, in the way that Ali and Elvis are characters of consequence – something in the beauty and the bones of these lives elevates biography into apologue.

96

20

Kilimanjaro, at 19,710 feet . . . is said to be the highest
mountain in Africa. Its western summit is called the
Masai 'Ngaje Ngai', the House of God. Close to the
western summit there is the dried and frozen carcass of a
leopard.

Ernest Hemingway, *The Snows of Kilimanjaro*

FROM 1974 THROUGH to the end of the decade nearly all
martial arts magazines in the US contained ads for
coloured T-shirts emblazoned with a cartoon illustration
of Lee's image and the wishful proclamation *Bruce Lee
Lives*.

We have the impression, when watching his movies,
that he arrived fully actualized; he had always been Bruce
Lee, the god of martial art. But even Hemingway's
leopard must have worked to reach the altitude at which
he fell, beautiful and damned.

Lee was born in San Francisco in 1940. His parents
named him Li Jun Fan and, as was customary then, a
Caucasian nurse arbitrarily entered the Christian name
Bruce Lee on his birth certificate. His mother, Grace, the
youngest daughter of an influential Shanghai entrepre-
neur, was half-German; his father, Lee Hoi Chuen, a
popular and wealthy Hong Kong comic performer and
movie actor (in the 1993 Hollywood hagiography,
Dragon: The Bruce Lee Story, Lee's father is anonymous,
widowed and nearly impoverished), was touring the USA

as a major performer with a Peking opera troupe.

Bruce Lee's had been a show-business family for many generations. The elder Lee arranged his son's first part in a movie: Bruce Lee appeared in a Hong Kong picture when he was three weeks old; he was six when his father helped him get his first starring role.

Lee grew up in his parents' home on the Kowloon side of Hong Kong, not, as was claimed in *Dragon*, as an only child, but with two brothers (one older, one younger), two sisters (one older, one younger), a pet monkey and several servants. The adolescent Bruce Lee was frisky and mischievous; his family's Cantonese nickname for him translates as 'Never Sits Still'.

Throughout the 1970s, I regarded Lee in the same way most fans still think of him: as the character in *Enter the Dragon* – a man alone, attuned to the natural world and his inner rhythms, a man clean of secondary wisdom. The historical Lee admired and was influenced not so much by Shaolin monks as by Elvis, James Dean and Jerry Lewis – whose facial expressions and body habits are observable in Lee's childhood movies as well as in the films he made as an adult – and by Chinese movies about kung fu masters. By his eighteenth year, Lee was a teen idol in Hong Kong and had starred in twenty films (none about martial arts), the most popular of which was *The Orphan*, in which he played a troubled adolescent in the James Dean mould.

At thirteen he began to study wing chun gung fu (the Cantonese pronunciation of kung fu, which Lee himself used). Movie lore has it that he was a quick and obsessive student. In actuality, he was more interested in acting, in girls, though he was basically shy with them, and in dancing – he became the cha-cha champion of Hong Kong – and didn't take a serious interest in wing chun until he was sixteen.

It has always been written that Lee studied gung fu

directly under Yip Man, the aged, esteemed head of the wing chun clan. As evidence, we have the famous photo of the venerated old opium smoker standing to the left of his fifteen-year-old pupil, smiling benevolently and looking as ancient, leathered, wise, foetal and transcendent as a mummy. Yearbook picture notwithstanding, old Professor Yip supervised senior students and instructors; Bruce Lee was not one of these. Indeed, all the indications are that Lee never had a single lesson with Master Yip. The future king of gung fu's primary teacher was Wong Shum Leung, who describes the one fight in which he saw the teenage Lee participate:

'We had contests on rooftops with other gung fu schools. These were common in Hong Kong and were not dangerous. One time we took Bruce along with the seniors. He did OK in the first round, but then said that he didn't want to fight. "I wanta go home," he said.

'We told him if he didn't go back in there, we'd show him what real fighting was – he'd have to fight us. He was scared, but he went back and finished his opponent fast.'

Bruce Lee legend tells this quite another way. According to popular myth, in his late teens, the apprentice god of martial art regularly fought in organized, weekly, illegal rooftop contests not dissimilar to seedy backroom bare-knuckle boxing smokers. Lee soon became the baddest boy in the Crown Colony. In his final rooftop battle, his opponent's skull was fractured. Since Lee was a well-known delinquent, police knocked on the door of Lee Hoi Chuen asking questions; the elder Lee saved face and Bruce Lee's life (a rival gang would surely kill his famous, street-hard son), by banishing him to the United States. These fables are indicative of much that devotees believe they 'know' about Lee.

The reality of how Lee came to the United States more closely resembles this: his influential dad didn't think the boys that waggish young Bruce had begun hanging out with were good influences. It would best serve his impetuously curious son to move to the USA and stay with upstanding family friends in San Francisco.

In most ways, Bruce Lee's adjustment to life in the States was not unconventional for a Hong Kong Chinese immigrant. Within weeks of arriving, he left San Francisco for Seattle, where he struggled to improve his English and get a high school degree at Edison Technical Institute; he later attended the University of Washington as a philosophy major; he excelled in some classes, and managed to survive most others, partly by trading gung fu lessons with better all-round students who agreed to write papers for him. He found a wife at university (not the sexually aggressive, genius cheerleader in *Dragon*, but a timid and inexperienced, sweet and sleepy-looking co-ed named Linda Emery), he quit school and along the way made a decision that was not at all conventional: he was going to become the best martial artist in the history of the world. Best. Ever. Period. No contest. Amen.

At gung fu demonstrations in Seattle Lee attracted the same sorts of people who would later become his most obsessive movie fans. 'Tough guys *and* wimps flocked to Bruce,' says Jesse Glover, Lee's first Seattle pupil.

Although *Dragon* and numerous Hong Kong movies perpetrate the Lee myth that he was a brilliant and anxious martial arts instructor, the historical Lee reluctantly began to teach mostly because he needed money and didn't want a job to get in the way of his own martial training. 'He didn't have the patience to teach,' explains Jim DeMile, another Seattle student. 'Bruce was a self-serving guy. He didn't see a reason to teach. He used us to improve his own skills, which isn't the same as teaching.'

Lee and wife moved to Oakland, California, in 1963, looking for a better market to make money from gung fu.

100

On 1 February 1965, the last day of that year of the dragon, a son, Brandon, was born. Lee opened a gung fu school near San Francisco's Chinatown. In the 1960s gung fu was basically unknown to Westerners. Many Chinese practitioners taught only other Chinese (as much because Chinese were the only ones interested as because of their legendary ethnocentricity). People from numerous ethnic backgrounds came to Lee. He taught anyone he wanted, he and his pupils wore street clothes when they practised, and he had no ranking system – his students wore no black and coloured belts. What's more, Lee was not shy about his belief that, to teach, he didn't need the support or approval of elders in the San Francisco Chinese community.

Concerned that they had lost face, those elders sent a representative to confront him. 'This guy came into Bruce's school,' explains Dan Inosanto, a long-time Lee pupil. 'He said, "If you beat me, you can teach. If I beat you, you got to close your school." '

In *Dragon*, this encounter is recreated as a high-kicking duel to the death between two screaming, posing, gymnastic athletes as hard-bodied, fierce and lethal as human-sized yellowjackets. Lee is paralysed by his evil, dirty-fighting opponent (who uses precisely the sort of tactics the historical Lee would have) and becomes depressed until he is coaxed out of his funk by the always beautiful and eternally optimistic Linda, who reinvigorates his shattered will and inspires him to write a brilliant philosophical treatise, named *The Tao of Jeet Kune Do*, about his transcendent martial art. This manuscript is published, almost overnight, as a respected mainstream book; its success and his wife's constant ministrations motivate Lee miraculously to cure his own paralysis.

This Hollywood revision trivializes not only Lee's life – as well as our concepts of love, work, art and serious illness – but his effect on the martial arts. My experiences as a sixteen- and seventeen-year-old in a Western North Carolina karate class were not unique. Before Lee, the vast majority of martial practitioners all over the world were basically incapable of defending themselves; athletes as we think of them in the West simply didn't exist in the Asian fighting disciplines.

'When we fought in tournaments and in schools,' says first world heavyweight kick-boxing champion and former Lee student, Joe Lewis, 'we tried to imitate real fighting by throwing what were supposed to be killing blows. We'd fire one kick or punch and wouldn't hit nothing, then stop and wait for the ref to call a point. There was no tactical movement, no defence to speak of, and no credit for how tough you were or weren't – because nobody was getting hit. More than anything, it was a game of tag. How can you call that fighting?'

In the real-world version of Lee's Oakland scrap, his puny, timid, underqualified opponent turned and ran as Lee chased him around a room. With closed fists (because he didn't know better), Lee pounded the back of his challenger's head. Lee's hands became painfully swollen and, gasping for breath, he tackled his opponent, pinned down his arms and sat on him.

Although Lee had 'won' this encounter, it woke him up (*What if this guy had been a* real *meanass?* Lee must have wondered), and brought on a period of considerable introspection. With what was as much shaky-ego bolstering and an obsession for success as a passion for knowledge, he began a process of reading, ruminating and training: of what has been described as moment-by-moment reinvention.

Over the next few years Lee became the first Western-style athlete in the martial disciplines. He ran, pushed weights, jumped rope, performed staggering numbers of callisthenics, punched numerous kinds of bags, developed dozens of pieces of training equipment he used daily –

many of which, after his death, were adopted by the burgeoning community of martial arts practitioners.

'No one ever trained as fanatically as Bruce,' says Chuck Norris, who became one of Lee's pupils. 'He seemed to train twenty-four hours a day.'

This ongoing sojourn in the internal wilderness became the basis of the revolution that Lee would lead in the martial arts. (In the mid- to late-1970s, like lots of guys, I spent hundreds and hundreds of dollars on equipment I believed Lee might have used or invented. I opened every corrugated paper box that arrived from martial arts supply companies as if it protected the martial equivalent of the Dead Sea Scrolls.)

Bruce 'Never Sits Still' Lee had adopted the distinctly American faith: that we can invent ourselves on a daily basis. And that we can work to become whatever and whomever we want.

He gave a demonstration of his method, which he called *Jun Fan* gung fu, named after himself, at a martial arts tournament in Los Angeles. Film of that demo was shown to *Batman* television series producer William Dozier, who called Lee in for a screen test and eventually cast him as Kato in *The Green Hornet* TV series.

In the spring of 1966 the Lee family moved to Los Angeles, where a daughter Shannon was born and twenty-six episodes of *The Green Hornet* were filmed. The show ran on ABC for one season. It was the first time Chinese martial art had been broadcast on national network American television. *The Green Hornet* series brought Lee to the attention of American martial practitioners, most of whom had not heard of him. 1967 Pan American Games judo gold medalist Hayward Nishioka describes seeing Lee on television. 'As soon as he came on, you knew he knew his stuff. For the first time ever on TV or in the movies, it wasn't hokey, it wasn't fake, it wasn't trick photography. It was real moves being executed with excellence.'

Karate competitor Bob Wall, who would later co-star with Lee in two movies, reinforces Nishioka's reaction. 'Because of Bruce, everybody I knew in the martial arts were fans of *The Green Hornet*. Nobody, and I mean nobody, missed the show. We wished it was *The Bruce Lee Show*, and he'd be fighting in every frame.'

Respected veteran stuntman Gene LeBell, who regularly worked on *The Green Hornet*, has his own, less enthralled, way of describing Lee and his role as Kato: 'Bruce was a driver that drove the stars around and wore a black outfit and a little hat.'

I, too, saw Lee in 1966, though it would be late 1973 before I'd remember having done so. Daddy, Carol and I were visiting an aunt, uncle and cousins in Charlotte. The Saturday morning after Thanksgiving, we drove from Uncle John's house on the outskirts of the city to the Christmas parade downtown. The sky was clear and bright. From Uncle John's third-floor office window, we stared down on the procession of clowns, cowboys on horseback, high school marching bands, and civic officials and beauty queens wearing thick overcoats, who waved and smiled and blew steam into the air from convertibles. Twenty minutes into the show, an innocuous white float passed our building. Several people were standing on the float, waving to kids and parents who lined the streets. The smallest person on the float was standing at the very front, by himself. He was wearing a black suit and mask, shiny gloves and a billed hat; he was waving his right arm and, like everyone else, his breath disappeared in the air.

'Who's that?' I asked my cousin Brent.

'That's Kato,' he replied. 'On TV.'

I didn't give the guy on the float another thought. Nothing about Bruce Lee felt cool or important or even interesting on that cold Friday morning in November 1966.

Lee himself was not keen on his co-starring role in *The Green Hornet*. He wanted to make 'real' movies, be a 'real' actor. Although he was frustrated by the robotics of playing Kato (before and since Lee, martial arts characters on TV and in the movies have always been less than human and little more than fighting robots, even when cast in lead parts) and his subsequent lack of acting jobs, he didn't despair. Linda took a job as a secretary, which allowed her husband the opportunity to commit himself yet more rigorously to his aspiration to become the world's most complete fighter.

'She gave him what he wanted,' explains James Coburn, who was a friend, benefactor and one of Lee's Los Angeles pupils. 'She left him alone, gave him comfort when he needed it, had children, and did everything for them. It kept him free. There was a kind of Asian subservience to it.'

Where most martial practitioners in the world slavishly followed one style of combat or another, Lee analysed and experimented with dozens of Eastern combat systems, including numerous styles of gung fu and karate, as well as tae kwon do, judo and jujitsu, and Western boxing, wrestling, and fencing (which Lee became interested in because his older brother Peter was accomplished with a foil), and the French foot-fighting sport, *savate*. His stated goal was to distil the essence – that which was most efficient and practical – from each martial system.

Chief among Lee's influences: Muhammad Ali. Lee, whose primary fighting stance was right-side forward, where Ali faced left, bought film of every Ali bout that he could find. Watching Ali's image through mirrors so he could more easily understand what Ali was doing, Lee attempted to emulate Ali's movements. In *Enter the*

Dragon, as Lee danced around a shocked-from-his-socks then knocked-on-his-twat Bob Wall, he was trying to replicate both Ali's footwork and facial expressions. And, like Ali, the Bruce Lee in *Enter the Dragon* always wore white or black or a combination of the two. (This style, this perceived relationship with Ali – and, therefore, me – was not a small part of what first pulled me to Lee.) 'Bruce idolized Ali, his brilliance, his footwork, his speed, his fluidity, his elusiveness,' says Joe Lewis. 'He felt that Ali was the best there was.'

Chunks of Lee's movie fight with Chuck Norris in *Way of the Dragon*, in which he makes Norris look like so much grey cubed steak being broiled on a jet-air grill – Lee bounds about a stationary Norris, coming down from his toes to blister Norris with a phantasm of too-quick-to-count punches – are lifted almost exactly from moments in the second and third rounds of Ali's *real* bout with Cleveland Williams and the third-round knockout in the Brian London fight. Or, more precisely, from television camera angles of the Ali–Williams and Ali–London contests.

Says Lewis: 'Bruce'd play the Williams fight over and over on that little eight-millimetre movie projector he had. First round, Ali's purposely *just* out of range; round two, he catches Williams mid-range; round three, Ali kisses him good night. Bruce went over this again and again. We'd study the way Ali punched, the way he moved, his ability to control an opponent even while backing up. Bruce emphasized mobility. Karate people were using stationary stances. One of the keys to defensive superiority is not to give your opponent a stationary target. Ali did that better than anyone. He was Bruce's hero until the day Bruce died.'

UCLA and Los Angeles Lakers basketball legend Kareem Abdul Jabbar, another of Lee's Hollywood students, says, 'Bruce was in awe of Ali. He said he wanted to train Ali how to kick. Bruce said if he could do that, Ali'd be on another planet.'

Wing chun had few kicking techniques; the kicks Lee would have used in combat would have been thrown (sensibly) to the ankles, knees, groin and coccyx. Throughout the 1960s Lee developed not only his street-fighting skills, but a spectacular, high-kicking, movie martial art. Coburn explains further. 'Bruce sucked up everything he could apply to his art. If it worked, it worked. If it didn't, out it went. All philosophers, all training, all teaching, everything. If it works, you do it. And you only find out if it works *by* doing it. The rest of it's all jive.'

Lee called his street-fighting method *jeet kune do*, which translates most accurately as *stop fist way*, though it usually has been translated, less meaningfully, as 'way of the intercepting fist'. Lee's movie martial art is often incorrectly referred to as *jeet kune do*.

'There are three opportunities to strike an opponent,' he said. 'Before he attacks, during his attack, or after he attacks.' In the *jeet kune do* of the mid-1960s, Lee attempted to focus on pre-attack options, the naïve notion being that the fighter who moves most economi-cally and efficiently, in a properly anticipatory fashion, will beat his opponent to the punch. (Yeah, OK, but what happens after that, when the guy doesn't fall down?)

Eventually Lee regretted giving his art a name. 'I am all styles, yet I am no style,' he said. He had labelled, and thereby limited, that which he thought of as limitless, formless, beyond definition.

'He says JKD has no technique,' Inosanto notes. 'My wife says everybody in the sixties talked that way.'

Like all of us, the 'limitless, formless' Bruce Lee was an ambiguous character driven by his biology, his culturiza-tion, and his time: the 1960s and 1970s, that phase when self-invention – the notion that you can cut yourself loose from psychic and physical moorings and float free, beyond the pull of gravity – seemed most possible.

I slowly stand, step to the mirrors and leap into a jumping spinning crescent-kick. When I should plop to the floor, I keep levitating up. I cross my legs, close my eyes, sit on the air and float.

On a trip to Bombay with Coburn and Siliphant, Lee visited a school that taught a traditional Indian martial art. The class had not heard of him. After he gave an impromptu demonstration dressed in street clothes, the amazed instructor and his pupils bowed to Lee on hands and knees. One can't feed two kids and a wife, though, by being placed on a pedestal as the god of gung fu. And the unemployed actor found it necessary to return to the role of martial arts instructor.

Lee had never particularly enjoyed teaching, but now he was bored with it. He wanted to showcase his mushrooming skills before a larger audience than he'd attract to a martial arts class; he felt that he needed, and deserved, to be internationally famous. To Lee, the best way to accomplish this would be to educate the entire world to Eastern culture and his ideas of what martial art should be – while validating his own shining existence.

Bruce Lee knew one place to seize this shimmering future. The place he knew was the perfect, the obvious, the only vehicle which could transport his martial art to the world. Bruce Lee, child of he movies, whose ideals of a gung fu master came from films he'd loved as a child, made the decision to pursue his singular art in this singular way: he'd become the world's best-known martial artist by becoming the first genuinely international movie star.

In 1969, inspired by a mail-order course from self-motivational speaker Napoleon Hill, Lee wrote a letter to himself. 'I, Bruce Lee, will be the highest-paid ... superstar in the United States. In return, I will give the most exciting performances and render the best of quality in the capacity of an actor. Starting in 1970, I will achieve world fame and from then onward till the end of 1980, I will have in my possession $10,000,000. I will live the way I please and achieve inner harmony and happiness.'

PART FOUR

THE SECRET DEATH OF AN AMERICAN DRAGON

He grows enormously
and begins to live   outside
of time
outside   of space
outside

of language   because

he's no longer here.

From a conversation with
Shelton Chow who paraphrases
A.E. Housman 'To an Athlete
Dying Young'

21

FROM THE LATE 1970s through to the early 1990s Brooklyn resident and documentary film producer George Tan travelled again and again from New York to Los Angeles to Seattle to San Francisco to Hong Kong. The purpose of Tan's quest: 'There was almost no valid information about the guy. I was looking for the real Bruce Lee, not some gung fu wizard. I followed the yellow brick road. Finally I reached Oz and found the man behind the curtain.'

One of Tan's basic discoveries on his fifteen-year odyssey, and what I found on my own sojourn, is this: 'In the history of movies,' says Tan, 'there's never been anyone else like Bruce. If Clint Eastwood had been a sheriff who became Christian about the whole thing and decided to show real sheriffing and had chosen movies as the medium, you could compare that to Bruce Lee.'

From 1967 to 1971, Lee taught many notables in the film community, including, among others, James Coburn, Blake Edwards, screenwriters Stirling Siliphant and Joe Hyams, Steve McQueen, Lee Marvin, Elke Sommer, Sharon Tate, Roman Polanski and Warner Brothers president, Ted Ashley. For those connected with the industry, those shepherds of the shimmering dream, Bruce Lee became the ideal of the martial monk, the wise man of gung fu. (It was also during this time in Hollywood that Linda Lee came to adopt a particularly reverential stance towards her husband, sitting beside him, silently mouthing his words as he spoke.)

'Now, when I look at photos of Bruce and Linda together,' says Tan, 'him and those huge-ass forearms, her all long-limbed and gawky and repressed, what I see is not Master and Ms Martial Monk but Popeye and Olive Oyl. Bruce's philosophizing came when he needed to develop an image, a device to market his martial art. He realized that there was more to be made from philosophizing than from getting punched in the face.'

As Lee had incorporated elements from gung fu, boxing, judo, karate, et cetera, into his fighting methods, he looked to the writings of popular 1960s sages to develop 'his' philosophy. In addition to Napoleon Hill, he was taken with Zen rebel Alan Watts and anti-mystic J. Krishnamurti, who, at the age of ten in southern India, had been adopted by elders from the Theosophical Society, who believed him to be a resurrection of their messiah.

At thirty-four Krishnamurti renounced that role and spent the remainder of his ninety-one years delivering the message that, by their very nature, religions and organized philosophies are obstacles to truth. Aphorisms attributed to Lee, which are now echolaliacally quoted by his widow, students and numerous followers, were lifted directly from Krishnamurti's work.

'Truth is not something dictated by your pleasure or pain,' wrote Krishnamurti, 'or by your conditioning as a Hindu or whatever religion you belong to. The man who is really serious, with the urge to find out what truth is, what love is, has no concept at all. He lives only in what is.'

The Tao of Jeet Kune Do is not, as was claimed in *Dragon*, the masterwork greatly influenced by Linda Lee as a twenty-three-year-old Bruce Lee lay paralysed in a hospital. It's an ongoing collection of notes that Lee did not intend to publish, but which were posthumously by his still-enthralled widow. In these notes Lee wrote, 'Fighting is not something dictated by your conditioning as a kung-fu man, a karate man, a judo man, or what not. The man who is really serious, with the urge to find out what truth is, has no (martial arts) style at all. He lives only in what is.'

Lee also created his wisdom from Chinese clichés (the 'pointing finger' analogy is an example) and adapted at least one of Mao Tse-tung's credos. 'Absorb what is useful; reject what is useless,' Mao said. Lee expanded this to include, 'Add specifically what is your own.'

To say that a person was not a great thinker, that he claimed others' thoughts as his own partly as a marketing ploy, is of course neither uncommon nor a crime. Nor do I mean to suggest that Lee didn't take these 'non-ideas' seriously. After all, he'd been interested in philosophy as an adolescent, had majored in it at university, and later collected such books about it by the hundreds, as well as any and all new and old volumes he could find about martial arts, boxing, wrestling and film-making. Lee's martial library consisted of thousands of books, many of which were long out of print and rare, which he annotated and cross-annotated with personal training notes.

'I saw Bruce as a renegade Taoist priest,' says a chuckling Kareem Abdul Jabbar. 'He was into spirituality and it was heavily influenced by Taoism. But you couldn't put him in that little box, he was beyond all that.'

George Tan has a different take on Lee. 'Bruce liked to use the word "Tao"; he used it over and over,' says Tan. 'And the commonly held view is that Bruce was *sort of* Taoist. The truth, in a lot of ways, is he was more Confucian. Taoists surf the waves; the basic idea of Taoism is to accept the world as it is. Taoists don't blow their horns in traffic. Confucians manipulate the world; they think it's here to serve them, not much different from the way Christians believe they reign over everything else. Bruce is a guy who believed he had somewhere to go – and he *had* to get there quick. He wasn't about to let anybody get in his way. Bruce was a Confucian in Taoist clothing.'

To support his role as the non-master master, Bruce Lee, the 'I'm above competition' Taoist marketing guru, recruited the three most successful American sport karate competitors of the 1960s as *his* students. He offered private instruction to Joe Lewis, to Chuck Norris and to Mike Stone.

Lewis gives Lee considerable credit for his success as a sport fighter. 'When I began working with Bruce, I became a much better competitor. I won ten consecutive grand championships without a loss. That was unheard of then and, hell, it's unheard of today. And what Bruce showed me enabled me to do that.'

'Fighting, as is, is simple and total,' Lee wrote. 'The core of understanding lies in the individual mind, and until that is touched everything is uncertain and superficial. After all, knowledge in the martial arts ultimately means self-knowledge.'

In the years since Lee's death the notion that we can be whatever we want, that we can liberate ourselves, has become the stuff of corporate advertising, of the self-help genre of non-writing, of government-sanctioned propaganda, of half-hour infomercials. In the early 1970s the concept of self-actualization seemed shining and new.

As the aggressively self-actualized Bruce Lee employed his relationships with Lewis, Stone and Norris to establish and then support his reputation as the world's premier professor of the fighting disciplines, Bruce Lee the performer used movie-industry students to try to convince major Hollywood producers that martial arts scenes would have more sizzle than 'ham-fisted' John Wayne-style saloon fights. Although celebrity pupils, particularly Stirling Siliphant, helped him get parts on several TV shows, including, among others, *Longstreet*, *Ironsides* and *Blondie*, no one took this little Chinese fellow seriously enough to give him a chance as a star.

'Never sits still.' Never gives up. In 1970 Lee had a story idea called *The Warrior* about a Shaolin priest's adventures in the American West, which he took to friends at Warner Brothers, including producer Fred Weintraub, who liked the idea and wrangled money to create a ninety-minute pilot for television.

Around this time, Lee wrote a rhyme for his friend Jhoon Rhee and mailed it to him in Washington, DC.

> Am I a giant among men,
> Master of all I survey.
> Or an ineffectual pygmy
> who clumsily blocks his own way?
>
> WHICH ARE YOU?
>
> The doubters said,
> 'Man cannot fly,'
> The doers said,
> 'Maybe, but we'll try,'
> And finally soared
> Into the morning glow,
> While non-believers
> Watched from below.

So damn the torpedo. full speed ahead! Remember what this Chinaman say, 'Circumstances? Hell! I make circumstances!'

Peace and inner harmony, Bruce

Lee told James Coburn that on a regular one-hour television series he could take the necessary time to educate viewers to his philosophy and his art. This is something he'd never be able to accomplish in movies, he said. Lee boasted to American martial arts magazine editors that Warner Brothers had offered him the lead in his own series.

What he didn't know is this: 'He came into my office swinging his nunchuks and jumping up and down for what must've been ten minutes,' says a former Warner Brothers television executive. 'We never seriously considered him for the role.'

Lee's story idea eventually became the *Kung-fu* TV series, which in the dubious tradition of Fu Manchu, Charlie Chan and Mr Moto, starred Caucasian non-martial artist David Carradine, who, week after week, shuffled across deserts and through cowtowns in varying states of consciousness. Tan says of the series, 'What was passed off as Taoism and Buddhism were writers' childhood Torah teachings filtered through West Coast big bucks and pseudo-hippie aesthetics.'

Carradine's character on the show was Chinese gung fu master Kwai Chang Caine, the role the world's most relentlessly conditioned Chinese martial arts practitioner had conceived – and coveted – for himself, but for which he received no credit.

In April 1970 Lee returned to Hong Kong to visit his mother and brother Robert (his father had died in 1965). For the first time *The Green Hornet* was playing in Hong Kong and Lee was surprised to find that he was *almost* a celebrity, a minor hero. He had left Hong Kong a well-known problem child and had returned transformed, enlightened, a master of a new form of gung fu (martial art is as revered by the Chinese as Christianity was by sixteenth-century Puritans), a local boy who had 'made good' on the fabled Gold Mountain of Hollywood.

Lee appeared with four-year-old son Brandon on the

Hong Kong television talk show, *Enjoy Yourself Tonight*, where the audience oohed and aahed over an uncommonly charismatic and board-shattering demonstration of his martial art, and where Lee introduced his heretical fistic philosophy to knowledgeable Hong Kong viewers. Twelve-year-old David Lo, movie director Lo Wei's son, was watching the show. The younger Lo excitedly told his father about Lee's demonstration.

Lo Wei remembered Lee from *The Orphan* and from several other films. Lo called the head of Hong Kong's fledgling Golden Harvest studios, Raymond Chow, to tell him about Lee. Chow, a runaway executive from the powerful Shaw Brothers Studio, was regarded by his former benefactor, Run Run Shaw, as a renegade and an outlaw. Not a bad fit for gung fu rebel Bruce Lee.

Shortly after Lee returned to Los Angeles from Hong Kong (at almost exactly the time he realized he'd always be treated as a second-class citizen in Hollywood), Chow offered a two-picture deal for $7,500 per movie, which Lee would accept.

Says Tan, 'With the release of his first movie, *The Big Boss* (retitled *Fists of Fury* for US distribution in 1972), Bruce became as big a celebrity in Hong Kong as the Beatles had been in England.'

The reason: 'His vitality was extraordinary,' says Fred Weintraub, who produced *Enter the Dragon*. 'No one had ever seen anything like Bruce. The life force was just staggering.'

22

IN 1971, *THE BIG BOSS* and Lee's second movie, *Fist of Fury* (later renamed *The Chinese Connection* in the United States), kicked the stuffings out of box-office records throughout south-east Asia. In Singapore showings were postponed because of traffic jams caused by fans. Throughout the Orient both movies played continually for nearly ten years.

'We are not the sick men of Asia,' Lee's screen character proclaimed to Japanese persecutors in *Fist of Fury*. With this single declaration (scripted by Lo Wei), several thousand punches and kicks, and an avenging-tomcat-from-hell battle scream created expressly for this picture, Bruce Lee transcended pop idol status and came to be regarded as a messiah not only by millions of Hong Kong Chinese, but eventually by hundreds of millions of put-upon people throughout the world.

By the time Lee completed his third picture, the self-written, -directed and -produced *Way of the Dragon*, he was developing the reputation, at least in Asia, that he'd been seeking, as the greatest fighter on the planet.

In early 1972 Lee brought his wife and children to Hong Kong from Los Angeles. After they'd settled in, he all but ignored them. Says Tan, 'By then, he was getting all the adulation he could want. He had alternative sources of affection.'

Where, in the States, Lee had effectively been a sexual neuter, Hong Kong women found him irresistible. They regarded him as worldly, mysterious, scholarly, sensitive, as the equivalent of the male ideal in Western romance novels. He took at least one mistress; other lovers included co-stars. In Hollywood Lee had worn khaftans, dashikis and Nehru jackets. In Hong Kong he bought a floor-length mink coat, Elvis-style sunglasses, a red Mercedes convertible. Worldwide, he became a legend among martial arts students. Larry Tan, who would later become a kung fu teacher and choreograph martial arts fights for several American movies, including *Remo Williams* and *The Wanderers*, describes an unexpected 1972 meeting with his childhood idol.

'There's never been anything in America like Bruce's fame in Hong Kong. He was on the cover of every single magazine – men's, women's, family magazines, it didn't matter. I saw him coming out of a restaurant. I'm at the bottom of these steps waiting for him to come down, waiting to meet my hero. I'm expecting a warrior-monk, this character out of his movies. What I got was Mr Vegas.

'His cologne – it's so overpowering I smell him before I see him. The first thing I see is this pair of four-inch platform heels. He's wearing bell-bottoms, this flowery shirt and jacket, huge sunglasses. I couldn't believe how tiny he was. Now, as an adult, I look back and see he was this little insecure guy who'd transformed himself onscreen into a physical giant.'

In mid-1972 Lee starred in, wrote, co-produced and directed the supposedly autobiographical *Way of the Dragon*, in which he played a bumpkin who's a gung fu genius. In Hong Kong and Taiwan *Way of the Dragon* quickly became known as Lee's religious affirmation of his own Chineseness. (In China the chief religion is not Taoism or Buddhism. Nor is it Confucianism or Maoism. The main religion among Chinese *is* Chinese, the religion of being Chinese, as being Jewish means more to those who are Hebrew than simple religion and ethnicity.) *Way of the Dragon* cemented Lee's Hong Kong reputation, and later his reputation worldwide, as a populist, a hero of common folk.

Lee choreographed all the fights for *Way of the Dragon*, easily the most substantive and real-seeming of his movie battles, many of which are remarkable even after hundreds of viewings (the short fight with Bob Wall, just before his more famous contest with Chuck Norris, has a particularly powerful verisimilitude to it); he also dubbed English voices on to the Mandarin soundtrack, and played percussion for the score.

Privately he studied the complex rhythms of Hindu music, hoping to apply them to the flow of combat and of fight-scene choreography; he experimented with electric shock to speed his reaction time; had the sweat glands removed from under his arms because he didn't like the way his dripping pits looked onscreen; drove open fingers into closed steel cans of cola. He said that, before the end of 1973, he'd plunge his fingers *through* pine boards – a feat which surely had never been accomplished. After his death boards would be found in his home with dramatic indentations in the wood.

He began receiving movie offers from around the world and told friends that he'd become an emissary for global harmony. Bruce Lee, the bringer of international-ism, the harbinger of one-world culturization that must take place in the twenty-first century.

Never sits still. Always reinventing. He wanted his next movie, *Game of Death*, to be a philosophical non-sermon about the necessity of being personally adaptable as a warrior, as well as a person. He planned to open the movie with a shot of a cedar bough breaking under weight of snow, followed by one of a river reed bending in the wind.

He wrote in letters to friends that he'd return to live in Hollywood and that he'd move his privately trained school of stuntmen, which included the likes of Jackie Chan and Samo Hung, with him. There were rumours that, after his return to the States, he would divorce Linda.

'He'd been drinking cow blood,' says Coburn, who visited Lee in Hong Kong in late 1972, 'spun in the blender, running seven miles a day. His skin was like very thin velvet – you could see every muscle and every muscle, of course, was absolutely workable. It was like he could leap twenty feet in the air and stick on the wall and come down. That shining glowing velvet skin. He looked beautiful.'

I am all styles; yet I am no style. 'I use no way as way, have no limitation as limitation,' said Lee.

Bruce Lee was movie star, writer, stunt choreographer, director, producer, philosopher, marketing genius, revolutionary, little man's messiah. In his quest to become the complete person, warrior and healer, monk and lover, creature of intellect and of flesh and of spirit, he felt the need to be the best in the world at almost everything he undertook.

Then, something began to go terribly, inexplicably wrong.

DEATH OF THE DRAGON SCRIPT, page 67:

WE SEE: Lee removing his shirt before his fight with Chuck Norris in Way of the Dragon: *there's an aura around him; he glows with the certainty of his own invulnerability.*

NEXT, WE SEE: Lee less than six months later, in the opening fight from Enter the Dragon, *the last scene filmed for the movie.*

His skin looks stretched tight and he moves stiffly, mechanically. He's a figure in an El Greco painting – angular, elongated, ready to ascend into heaven.

23

By MID-1972 LEE was being prominently featured in almost every issue of Hong Kong's numerous daily newspapers.

Says Bob Wall, 'Wherever we were driving, they'd scream, they'd wave and squeal. It reminded me of clips I'd seen of Muhammad Ali and Elvis Presley getting mobbed. It was unbelievable, it was overwhelming.'

To prevent riots, department stores closed to allow Lee to shop by himself. When he wanted to go for a drive to relax, he was escorted by motorcycle police. It was a by-product of Lee's martial training to be purposely para-noid. For years, he'd worked at being aware of move-ments of people who might attack him, to size up everyone in crowds. The eminently self-actualized Bruce Lee's martial fanaticism did not prepare him for the noose of super-celebrity.

In early 1971, when he was living in Los Angeles, Lee had weighed better than 145 pounds. By late 1972, he was down to 126; in April 1973, his doctor says that he was at 122. Lee said he'd purposely dropped weight, that lowering his percentage of body fat made him appear more muscular onscreen. 'Look at me,' he told Holly-wood student Ted Wong, who visited him in Hong Kong. 'Nothing but muscle and bones. I feel good, I'm strong.'

'Bruce's body must have been less than one per cent fat,' says Dr Donald Langford, the Lee family's physician in Hong Kong. 'It was obscene how little body fat he had.'

In the States, Lee had been playful and jovial, 'a practical joker and a cut-up', says Coburn, 'a clown', says Jabbar. In Hong Kong the unexpected pressures of celebrity left Lee insecure, tense, easily agitated.

'He became very paranoid,' Coburn says sadly. 'He had this impenetrable aura, this shield around him for ten, maybe twelve feet. Anybody who came within that area was real suspect and they had to watch out.'

Since his Hollywood days, Lee had been an occasional 'recreational' drug user. Now, in hopes of calming himself and relieving the choking level of stress he felt he was under, he regularly ate hashish brownies and leaves of marijuana. In Hong Kong he chose not to smoke the drugs, not wanting to damage his health.

He suffered greater paranoia, sleeplessness, memory loss. And headaches. He feuded with Coburn and Siliphant; sniped at McQueen, at co-workers, at fans, at 'ignorant' Hong Kong Chinese in general; he threatened to kill Bob Wall on an *Enter the Dragon* set. 'He was repeating himself,' says Wall sympathetically. 'He told me a story on the phone, then I went to his place and he told me the story twice more, every time like he'd never said it before. It was clear there was something wrong. I thought he was just plain overworked. But he was concerned. You could see he was concerned.'

Coburn laments the ways Lee changed in Hong Kong. 'He used to express so much joy. You know, that's a hard thing to express. For a man, anyway. Sometimes it happens in a woman. Bruce could arouse that joy in me. But that's the thing that had left. That left before he left.'

Ever since moving to Hong Kong, Lee had sent regular reports of his astounding successes to his former student, Ted Ashley, at Warner Brothers. Producer Fred Weintraub flew to Hong Kong to meet Lee on the set of *Game of Death*. In the fall of 1972 Lee and Weintraub signed contracts. Bruce Lee would get that for which he had striven for so long: he would make his first film for international audiences and would become a global star.

The proposed title of the picture was *Blood and Steel*, which Lee fought hard to change to *Enter the Dragon* – to signify his arrival. He stopped work on *Game of Death* to begin production of *Enter the Dragon*.

'I feel a power bubbling up inside me,' he said. It is this power – a beautiful lunacy – that we see roll from Lee in his *Enter the Dragon* fights.

'Bruce was very in touch with his own personal octane,' exclaims Jabbar, who worked with Lee on several fights for *Game of Death*. 'He could be there at the edge and he could get right to it. Bruce'd be white-hot in less than three-quarters of a second.'

'Intense is the first word that comes to mind,' *My Left Foot* and *Enter the Dragon* co-producer Paul Heller says when asked to describe Lee on the set. 'He could focus himself at any one thing more totally than anybody. He was more alive than anybody I've ever seen. His body – you could press and it was like hitting a piece of mahogany – there was no give anywhere.'

'That boy is crankin',' an LSD-stoned dorm-mate of mine said in September 1973 while staring hang-jawed at Lee in one of his more orgasmic *Enter the Dragon* battles.

Intense. Alive. White-hot. Crankin'. No give.

His best friend, James Lee, died in Oakland; Yip Man passed away in Hong Kong. Director Robert Clouse's wife says that during the filming of *Enter the Dragon* Lee told her he would be dead before his next birthday.

Principal photography for *Enter the Dragon* was completed in April 1973. Lee edited fight scenes and dubbed his voice to the soundtrack, and went back to work on *Game of Death*. He'd become regarded as a mystically empowered fighter and was challenged through Hong Kong newspapers, as well as on the streets, by would-be usurpers.

Tales of these duels are no less the stuff of myth than theories about his death. An often-told legend has it that as a guest on *Enjoy Yourself Tonight*, upstart Lee was noisily beckoned by an elderly kung fu master to try to push him out of his strongest fighting stance. According to the story, Lee rose from his seat, sauntered across the stage and punched the old man in the face. In Bruce Lee folklore the ancient master was knocked flat on the seat of his trousers. 'I don't push,' Lee reportedly said by way of explanation, 'I punch.' It would seem to be a perfect *jeet kune do* thesis.

There is, however, no film to confirm that this 'televised' exchange took place. And no one I've been able to find who worked on *Enjoy Yourself Tonight* remembers it. What's more, regardless of everything happening in his life, Lee would have had little reason to flatten some crotchety old man.

Fog and shadows.

'It was like *Gunfight at the OK Corral*,' claims Heller of Lee's encounters. 'They stand and tap their foot and you've got to take up the challenge. And Bruce would ignore it or walk away. Sometimes he couldn't. These were fierce encounters and the guys would get *hurt*. Bruce was so fast – he had reflexes and timing I defy anybody to this day to match.'

Mist and dreams.

Although most tales of Lee's Hong Kong battles have little more substance than television legends about Billy the Kid, it's true that newspaper ads offered movie contracts to the challenger who could dethrone the seemingly invincible Bruce Lee. Lee was involved in several real skirmishes. He side-kicked a hair stylist who challenged him on a *Fist of Fury* set and thumped two fistically ambitious stunt extras while *Enter the Dragon* was being filmed. More seriously, one aspiring kung fu hero apparently leapt the stone wall that enclosed Lee's Kowloon Tong home. Upon landing, he was afforded the uncommon privilege of getting folded by the right foot of Hong Kong's most legendary kick-fighter, then tossed from the property with a footprint across his abdomen.

Lee's student Herb Jackson says, 'This fella said to Bruce. "How good are you?" And Bruce was popping mad. "This guy invading my home, my own private home," he told me. Bruce said he side-kicked this guy harder than he'd ever kicked anyone. He gave it all to him.'

Gave it all. Lee, who signed Hong Kong fan photos 'Peace and Openness, Bruce Lee', push-pinned a black velvet poster above his desk in the study in his house. In the poster two cartoon vultures are perched atop a dead tree. 'Patience, Hell,' one vulture says to the other, 'I'm gonna kill somethin'.'

Lee was the only star who was coveted by studios all over the globe: Warner Brothers, which had shunned him less than eighteen months before, hoped to sign him to star in several films; Paramount wanted him, as did Italian, Taiwanese and other Hong Kong movie-makers.

Another reason Lee felt suffocated was that he had promoted Bruce Lee as the single deadliest human on the planet: he was sure he would eventually have to support this claim. The world's chief exponent of unarmed combat bought a handgun (all firearms were illegal in Hong Kong), which he carried with him when he left his house.

On 10 May, while at Golden Harvest dubbing his voice for *Enter the Dragon*, Lee collapsed and was rushed to hospital, near death. He suffered a series of full-body seizures and cerebral oedema. It was the next day before he regained full consciousness.

The first week of June the worried Lee flew to UCLA

Medical Center for further tests. His mother and brother now lived in Los Angeles. He stopped by the apartment they shared.

'He said he was wondering how much he could push his body,' says younger brother Robert. 'He's constantly pushing himself to higher levels. He's always out to find more knowledge. He said, "Oh, man, the doctor told me I got a body like an eighteen-year-old." And he was thin but he was in good spirits.'

Lee also spoke to James Coburn. ' "They told me I was in perfect shape, everything is cool. Just take it easy. Just take it easy for a while," ' Coburn quotes Lee as saying.

Returning to Hong Kong, Lee quit physical training, except for daily runs through his neighbourhood, and concentrated his energies on his movie career.

Six weeks later, on 20 July 1973, three weeks before the release of *Enter the Dragon*, Bruce Lee died.

PART FIVE

RIDING THE GHOST TRAIN

I have on my table a violin string. It is free.
I twist one end of it and it responds. It is free.
But it is not free to do what a violin string
is to do – produce music.

So I take it, fix it in my violin and
tighten it until it is taut.
Only then is it free
to be a violin string.

Rabindranath Tagore

24

WITHIN HOURS, LINDA Lee issued a statement that her husband had inexplicably collapsed while taking a walk with her in the garden outside their home. On 25 July, 25,000 people attended Lee's funeral, the largest in Hong Kong's history. His body was flown to the US for a second funeral; his pallbearers included McQueen and Coburn. Among others, Coburn, Ashley and Siliphant delivered eulogies. He was quietly buried in Seattle's Lakeview Cemetery, near Linda's mother's home.

Enter the Dragon was released on the second Friday in August.

On the basis of that one picture, Bruce Lee became a worldwide celebrity. Japanese teenagers cut their hair like his. Taiwanese eulogized him as 'Man with the Golden Singing Legs'. Thousands of martial arts schools sprouted up across Britain, Europe and the USA. Hundreds upon hundreds of fan magazines were published with fictionalized accounts of Lee's heroic deeds. Bruce Lee comic books and cartoons were produced and released in Asia. Tens of millions of people came to see Lee's movie fights as virtual religious artefacts.

Internationally, *Enter the Dragon* was Warner Brothers' highest grossing movie of 1973. A cinema in Iran played the film daily until January 1979, when Shah Pahlavi was overthrown by the Ayatollah Khomeini. Elvis bought a 35-millimetre copy of the movie and watched it dozens and dozens of times; inspired, he decided he would make his own martial arts film, which began production but was never completed. During the 1970s, *Enter the Dragon* was released again and again in the USA; each time, it landed among the top-five grossing pictures of the week. For nearly ten years, in major cities around the world, inner-city gang members turned out for *Enter the Dragon* with a similar ritualistic reverence to Catholics attending mass. As of the twenty-fifth anniversary of Lee's death, including worldwide video and television sales, *Enter the Dragon* had grossed over 400 million dollars and had been listed, for more than twenty years, as one of the twenty most profitable movies in the history of cinema.

On the day of Lee's Hong Kong funeral, the *South China Mail*, Hong Kong's largest English-language newspaper, disclosed that he had died, not with his wife, but in the apartment of movie actress Betty Ting Pei, with whom he'd been having an affair.

At a quickly arranged inquest, Ting Pei testified that Lee complained of a headache when he came to her apartment; she gave him a tablet of a prescription medication called Equagesic, the ingredients of which are 200 milligrammes of a common anti-anxiety agent (meprobamate) and 325 milligrammes of aspirin. After swallowing the Equagesic, Lee left Ting Pei and went to lie on her bed; when she tried to wake him, he couldn't be roused. Although Ting Pei testified that she checked regularly on Lee and that each time she did he appeared to be sleeping peacefully, when he arrived dead at Queen Elizabeth Hospital his hair was plastered to his head with sweat, his body and clothes were soaked through. A University of London professor of forensic medicine, R.D. Teare, who supervised the inquest jury, determined the immediate cause of death to be cerebral oedema: Lee's brain had become dramatically swollen and pressed against the inside of his skull. Teare added that the pain from such a death is usually 'exquisite and excruciating'.

Among other released findings – Lee had eaten cannabis not only on the day of his death, but shortly before his 10 May collapse. Professor Teare said that although there was no evidence that Lee had been murdered, his death appeared not to be from natural causes. He concluded that Lee's demise was not accidental but was, instead, a 'death by misadventure'. Teare and the inquest jury concluded that oedema had been caused by hypersensitivity to one or more of the ingredients in a single tablet of Equagesic.

25

'YOU'D ALMOST HAVE to use a ouija board to come by that conclusion,' says Dr Donald Langford, a former Baptist missionary and Lee's physician in Hong Kong.

'This man was muscled like a squirrel, spirited as a horse. I've never seen anybody as physically fit as Bruce. Equagesic is prescribed in the million dose every day in Asia. No analgesic killed Bruce.

'In my opinion, the cause of Bruce Lee's death is obvious. Every time I saw him after May 10th, he was further and further into his own hype. I don't think Bruce thought there was anybody in the world who knew what was good for him except Bruce Lee. That's what killed him. The same series of events that took place in May caused Bruce Lee's death in July. Bruce was particularly sensitive to one or more of the alkaloids in cannabis. He died from hypersensitivity to chemicals in cannabis or a cannabis by-product. Bruce's was a self-inflicted, though innocent, fatal illness.'

26

DR PETER WU, the respected neurosurgeon who saved Lee's life in May, agrees. 'I think that Bruce was fully convinced he was invincible, that he was immortal. This is what brought him down.

'He would have died in May from severe brain oedema,' says Dr Wu, who is renowned for his cerebral oedema research in Asian males. 'Bruce was in a very critical condition. It was sheer luck that experienced medical people were there to help him. We removed quite a lot of hashish from his stomach. In Nepal there have been all kinds of neurological problems associated with hashish, especially cerebral oedema. Bruce said that he was chewing the hashish because he was under a lot of pressure. Doing that, he would be exposed to all of the chemicals full strength. We gave Bruce a long talk before he was discharged from hospital, asking him not to eat the stuff again. We told him that his very low percentage of body fat could make him vulnerable to drugs. We said that the effects would be heightened by continued contact. We also told him that his level of stress could dramatically magnify the effects. Since he'd already had a very bad time with the drug, we told him the effects were likely to be worse the next time.

'He said that it was harmless. He said that Steve McQueen had introduced him to it and Steve McQueen would not take it if there was anything bad about it. I asked him if Steve McQueen was a medical authority. He didn't get my joke.

'To tell the truth, when Bruce left hospital, I thought he would be back. I had a very bad feeling about it.'

27

WHY HAVEN'T THESE opinions and this information been previously reported? Why wasn't hypersensitivity to cannabis part of the official verdict of the inquest jury?

'You have to understand something about Hong Kong Chinese culture,' explains Dr Langford. 'When Bruce's body was wheeled into the emergency room, all the Chinese vanished. It was difficult to find anyone to take care of him. The Chinese weren't about to be connected with, to be blamed for, the death of Hong Kong's most famous hero. It would have been regarded as a terrible loss of face.

'The same is true of the inquest: people weren't about to step up and say that Bruce Lee had died from eating cannabis or some related product. At the beginning of the inquest proceedings, Dr Wu and a couple of other doctors and I were pulled to the side and asked to play down the role of cannabis in Bruce's death.

'For years, I was suspicious this might have been some sort of cover-up. Now I realize that it was something else: they simply wanted to present a socially acceptable explanation. There was no recorded incidence of this drug as a cause of death. Hong Kong authorities felt that Bruce Lee's death had put them on the world stage. They were trying to avoid embarrassment, trying not to look silly. They didn't know that no one was watching. No one cared about Bruce Lee. Amazingly, not one single

Hong Kong reporter – or any reporter anywhere – ever interviewed me about Bruce or his death.'

28

WHEN LEE DIED, he was not wealthy. He left a wife and two children with one obvious means of financial support: two six-figure life insurance policies.

He'd signed statements, when he'd taken out the policies in 1972, that he'd never used any form of illegal drug.

Joe Lewis says, 'Hell, back in Hollywood, I saw Bruce doing dope right in front of me. One time he walked into my place and started passing out these huge joints the size of big cigars. I said, "Bruce, that's not the way you do it. You just roll one little one and pass it all around." He tells me, "No need to share. I want everyone to have their own." And he thumps his chest like he did in the movies, real audacious and proud. Everybody thought that was funny. That was Bruce, all right. Bruce to a T. But it's not like anybody thought anything was wrong with all that. It was the sixties and seventies. We thought it was innocent. Everybody was doing drugs.'

Coburn confirms Lee's Hollywood drug use. 'He'd want to get high and have a ball, listen to music. Blowing Gold was one of his favourite things.'

And Wall tells this story. 'I was in Bruce's study in Hong Kong while we were making *Enter the Dragon*. He kept the door to that room locked when he wasn't there. He had this plate of pot brownies sitting on the desk and while we're talking he kept eating brownies and offering them to me.'

Lewis remembers another anecdote about Lee which he regards as significant. 'There was this time in about 1969 that Bruce was at the house and my wife fixed him a drink. Some kind of sweet, syrupy thing. I don't remember what it was called, I don't drink. And Bruce drank it and then he got unbelievably sick. He turned red, he was sweating, sweat was running all down his face. And we helped him to the bathroom. He threw up and threw up and then threw up still more. It doesn't seem like such a mystery to me how Bruce died. Some people are just real sensitive to what they put in their bodies. And Bruce was one of those guys.'

Donald and Mary Langford lived in the same Kowloon Tong neighbourhood as Bruce Lee and his family, 'less than fifty yards from their estate', says Langford.

'Somewhere around midnight on the night Bruce died, Raymond Chow called. He was leaving the hospital with Linda, he said. He asked if they could stop by my house.

'When they got there about one o'clock, Linda was distraught. She didn't know what to do, what to tell reporters. This is a young, inexperienced woman who loved her husband and was enormously proud of him. He was becoming a big movie star and he was incredibly fit. She had no reason to believe she wouldn't have many, many years to spend with Bruce.

'Now there's this. Not only is he dead, but here she is with all these questions about this actress he died with. What's more, she has two young children to take care of – by herself. And she's in Hong Kong, where she can barely speak the language. Linda and I were in the same Cantonese class for Americans. She struggled with the language even more than I did.

'That night, in my living room, she asked what I knew about Bruce's relationships with women, whether or not he was a philanderer. I told her truthfully, to the best of my knowledge, that he had no other relationships.

'But Linda thought, quite accurately, that the Hong Kong press would devour her husband. Her major concern was how to keep tawdry things from being said. She handled herself with considerable poise and dignity during those times. I don't think that anyone could've done better than she did. I believe it was in my living room that she and Raymond Chow decided what statement they'd give to reporters.

'Personally, I'd have considerable sympathy for Linda if I knew she fictionalized an aspect or two of Bruce's demise, not only to protect his hero's image, but to get the money she felt was rightfully hers to raise those kids.'

In 1974 the two companies from which Bruce Lee had purchased life insurance wrote cheques to Linda Lee for half of the face value of those policies.

In the years following Lee's death, his reputation as a martial artist became badly damaged not only by Chopalong Wong imitators (many people believe that Bruce Li – whose real name is Ho Chun Tao – is Bruce Lee and that, instead of four movies, Lee made dozens), but by his own students.

Shortly before his death, Lee closed his Los Angeles, Seattle and San Francisco schools and demanded that his art not be taught by the three 'authorized' *jeet kune do* instructors, Dan Inosanto in Los Angeles, James Lee in Oakland, Taky Kimura in Seattle, or by any of Lee's other pupils.

George Tan explains Lee's motives. 'He felt no one was qualified. A lot of people who hung out with Bruce, especially during his Hollywood years, were weak men. Most of his students were guys he could use as moving, breathing punching bags. The exception was Jimmy Lee – but he died before Bruce. Bruce knew the lack of quality in his students and teaching would come back to haunt him.'

With Lee's death and the success of *Enter the Dragon*, former students, most of whom wanted honestly to perpetuate Lee's teaching methods, also recognized that considerable money could be made by claiming to be heirs to Lee's art. Says Tan, 'Bruce knew this would happen. It's like Christianity or most any other thing. First, along comes an innovator. He dies and the guys left behind are followers. Most of them don't have any real idea what Bruce was saying or doing, let alone the ability to execute it.'

In the post-Lee years, *jeet kune do* has become much of what Lee sought to change in the martial arts: it pretends to be free-flowing, but is structured, systematic, formulaic, unintentionally worshipful, paralysingly dogmatic. 'Lots of these JKD people sit around and play office politics,' Tan says, 'fighting each other for what they can make by marketing Bruce's bones as icons. Bruce was a revolutionary. He did his best to knock down the whole office building and grind up the bones of everybody inside. He's the guy who wanted to take a wrecking ball to the very *idea* of having an office building.'

Lewis agrees. 'If Bruce knew what some of these guys were teaching and calling JKD, he'd claw his way out of his grave to kick their shiny behinds. The *jeet kune do* crew has become a bigger bunch of pussies than any group I know of in the martial arts. *Jeet kune do*, my foot. *Geek kune do* is more like it. You try that stuff in a real fight, you might just get yourself hurt bad.'

On 31 March 1993, approaching the twentieth anniversary of Lee's death, his only son, Brandon Bruce Lee, was shot on a movie set in Wilmington, North Carolina. He died that evening and was buried beside his father in Seattle. The .44 calibre handgun with which the younger

Lee was shot was supposed to have contained blanks. It was the first time in the history of film that a leading actor had been shot and killed by a live-round on the set.

The younger Lee had wanted to admire his father, but had difficulty separating the myths he had heard from the breathing human being he had only known briefly. After his father's death, Brandon Lee was regularly challenged by schoolmates who'd learned that he was the son of Bruce Lee. 'Back then, we moved around a lot,' he said. 'I'd get to a new school and there'd always be somebody there trying to kick my ass.'

Brandon Lee had not wanted to perform martial art or to make action movies. He studied drama at Emerson College in Boston and took acting lessons in Manhattan in hopes of becoming a serious actor, but had little success getting roles, and eventually chose to take advantage of his unique heritage. He decided to jumpstart an acting career by making a few martial arts movies; he believed the success he'd find in those would allow him the opportunity to perform in quality dramatic projects both on the screen and on stage.

By early 1993 Brandon Lee had starred in one martial arts movie for a Hong Kong studio and two action features for American producers. He had multiple-picture deals with 20th Century-Fox and with Carolco Studios. The younger Lee was hard at work on his fourth film – the adult Bruce Lee, of course, completed four movies in which he was the star. Brandon had nearly finished work on his first vehicle for Carolco Studios, *The Crow*. In *The Crow* his role was that of a pop idol who has been resurrected to avenge his own murder. The scene being filmed when Brandon was shot was one in which his character is killed. It's not a dissimilar plot to many of the exploitative films about his father.

Legendary rumours about the father's death seemed ready-baked for the son's. (Crows are symbols of death in both the East and the West. Some Chinese are superstitious about the word 'death' being used in titles. One of the Asian fables about the elder Lee's demise was that the gods – or fate or karma or *something* – killed him for naming his work-in-progress, *Game of Death*.) The seeming relationship between the deaths of Bruce and Brandon Lee caused greater confusion about the elder Lee's exit; details became blurred, intertwined. Many people came to remember Bruce Lee as having been shot and murdered.

Within weeks of Brandon Lee's death, the son's story had become a footnote to the father's legend.

In 1993 and 1994, at public auctions, Linda Lee sold many of Bruce Lee's personal effects, including his business cards, his tank-tops and leather jacket, his wallet, his platform shoes. She gave the money from these sales to charities.

Among the few items that did not sell were Lee's handwritten notes and anatomical drawings for the fight scenes in *Way of the Dragon*, the screen bouts into which Lee put the most work and those with which he was most pleased.

'I was teaching this seminar at a karate school in Ohio,' says Lewis. 'The instructor had this pair of Bruce Lee's yellow sneakers – you know, the ones he wore in *Game of Death* ('completed' by Raymond Chow, with a Lee imitator, in 1977) – that he brings out and holds up in front of the students.

'In traditional karate schools, at the beginning of class, students bow to a Buddhist shrine. This guy's students bowed to these little yellow shoes. And then this teacher talks about the aura he feels around the shoes and leans over and tells me his students'll get proper martial energy from these old size-seven Cs.

'I found out the funniest thing later. This guy didn't know those sneakers weren't Bruce's. They were ones made for a Bruce Lee imitator after Bruce was dead.'

29

BEFORE THE NAME Bruce Lee is entirely enveloped by the mists of pop mythology, perhaps it would be useful to define what the person who breathed and fought and dreamed and died has left us.

Lee was the Frank Lloyd Wright of martial art. He was an original, who studied obsessively what had come before him, then reinvented the rules, in the hope of creating a universal, interconnected fighting form.

Lee's martial art was as unique as Wright's 'organic architecture', if not as roundly developed. (But then, Wright lived to be a very old man, who'd worked on his art for many decades.) In only a few years Lee revolutionized Asian fighting disciplines, made them 'organically' American and evangelized this product around the globe.

It's hard to overstate how visible the martial disciplines have become because of Lee. If he had not existed, few of us would have heard of martial art or kung fu. Before Lee's death there were fewer than 500 martial arts schools in the world; by the late 1990s, because of his influence, there were more than 20 million martial arts students in the United States alone.

'There isn't a martial artist on the planet who hasn't been influenced by Bruce,' Tan claims. And this seeming overstatement is probably true.

'Karate people all over the globe are light years further along than when Bruce was alive,' Lewis declares. 'For instance, a lot of guys in this country call the martial art they practise American freestyle. That way of thinking exists because of Bruce. He helped a whole lot of people jump out of some small boxes.'

In addition to Lee's considerable legacy of introducing more Westerners to Asian culture and philosophy than anyone else in history, he served to foreshadow, and be a forebear of, the hyperfitness body culture of the latter portion of our century. Before Lee, none of us had seen anyone with his steamlined, functional, no scrap muscularity. *How can anyone look like that?* I wondered, watching *Enter the Dragon*; in 1999, studying photos of him on my desk, it still seems almost impossible to me. Yet this aesthetic, first encountered in Lee, has since become not only desirable but is regarded as a twenty-first-century, new-evolutionary goal, among both men and women.

What's more, Lee fundamentally changed movie fight scenes: those of us born before 1960 grew up in a culture which considered kicking to be 'dirty' fighting; martial arts are now employed in nearly every fight in almost every action movie.

The best, and most successful, martial arts movie personality since Lee has been, of course, Jackie Chan, who had the distinction of being anonymously killed by Lee in both *Fist of Fury* and *Enter the Dragon*. Chan's onscreen comic kung fu genius/doofus persona was derived by Hong Kong producers partly from Lee's Tang Loong ('China Dragon') character in *Way of the Dragon*, far and away Lee's most popular movie in Asia. But no one, including Chan, has come close to recreating the verisimilitude, dramatic pacing and resonance of Lee's fights. What we've been left with post-Lee are such de-evolutionized by-products as *Teenage Mutant Ninja Turtles*, *Power Rangers*, Steven Seagal, Jean-Claude Van Damme and Sylvester Stallone, who patterned not only

Rocky boxing scenes but *Rambo*'s hypertrophic gunplay displays on Lee's movie battles.

And, more surprising than his influence on other fighting movie and television stars, if there had not been Bruce Lee movies, there might not have been a 'Sugar' Ray Leonard.

In the fall of 1979, I was attending East Carolina University in Greenville, North Carolina. In addition to taking creative writing classes and obsessively working to teach myself to write, I taught self-defence two nights each week and was still pretending to myself that I might become the world's greatest living martial artist.

In late November eastern North Carolina received its largest snowfall on record. The town of Greenville, where it usually snows no more than once every ten years, didn't have equipment to clear the roads. The university cancelled all classes. Public transport did not run.

Lyn and I had been married a little over a year. Drifts beside the house trailer we were renting measured deeper than six feet. For several days we weren't able to leave our trailer park. Being newly-weds, we did not mind.

It was while stranded in the snow that I first saw 'Sugar' Ray Leonard box. On the evening news there was an item about him training to fight Wilfredo Benitez for Benitez's world welterweight championship. The Benitez–Leonard contest would be broadcast live on Saturday afternoon. Anxiously I radared in on the bout. Leonard knocked out the previously unbeaten Benitez in the fifteenth round. His flashy, hands-dropping style indicated he'd learned much from Ali. But unlike Ali he was no force of nature. (*How could he be? I'd seen him sitting behind me in the Carolina Theater. I knew he was nothing but skin and blood and bones.*) And I had a fat enough ego to believe fully that, if given the chance, I could whup 'Sugar' Ray myself.

But time brings changes we can't expect. And in the 1980s I became quite a 'Sugar' Ray Leonard fan. When he fought at his best, Leonard was much as Terry Davis describes Pélé in his fine coming-of-age novel, *Vision Quest*. 'He can lift himself, and the rest of us sad-ass human beings, up to a better place, if only for a minute.'

When I finally began to make a writing career for myself in the late 1980s, three of the first four assignments I received from national magazines were about Ray. As I got the opportunity to spend time with him, we found we had some things in common. When we were kids we'd both collected comics by the hundred. As adolescents we'd worked to emulate Ali and Lee and were still big fans. After we became friendly, I mailed Ray several videocassettes of rare Lee footage which George Tan had sent me. When we spent time together, we often spoke about martial arts and discussed a couple of little-known facts about the foundation of Ray's ring skills: he says he learned much of his defence from watching Lee in movies; and, as Leonard trained for fights, during sparring rounds he often imitated Lee's alleycat-on-heat battle cries.

While writing a profile of Ray for the *Washington Post Magazine* before one of his final bouts, I planned to spend several days in his training camp. In that time I hoped he might afford me the opportunity to hop into the ring with him and move around a little.

For the first time in more than a decade, I started training not simply for the pleasure of working out, but to fight. In the early afternoon, for two full months, regardless of the weather, I went out to my garage, where I performed five hard rounds on the heavy bag, three on the speed bag, and shadow-boxed thirty straight minutes per session. As I danced about the bag, trying to rip through its canvas, I'd see Leonard's face in front of me. Not the Ray Charles Leonard I knew as an adult, the one

I'd often interviewed and whose ring skills and style I admired, but my seminal 'Sugar' Ray, the one with the rounded, shining halo of hair, the smarmy smile and the too-cute sailor suits, the one who as a late adolescent I had wanted to box and had felt I might humiliate.

I arranged to hook up with Ray on his fourth day of sparring. As I walked into his gym in Palmer Park, Maryland, on a Friday afternoon, he was already in the ring. There was nothing flashy about him today, no play in his demeanour. He was dressed in black trunks and gloves, a hooded basic black sweatshirt. He looked the way the older Ray Robinson might have looked, if Robinson had been a Druid.

Leonard peeled off his sweatshirt, revealing a plain white T-shirt soaked with sweat and cinnamon-coloured skin on his arms and neck. He paced around the ring a dozen times, luminous and quivering, aching with beauty. Which is to say that although Leonard is a fine-looking man, he was not born beautiful. He *creates* his beauty.

On this afternoon he's a ghost in the ring. He boxes with five different world-class fighters, none of whom can find him. Between rounds, he's jubilant. He and his trainer, Jose Pepé Correa, can't hide their smiles. 'Beautiful, beautiful,' Correa calls from the apron. 'Yes, yes,' he exclaims as his fighter continues to box with elegance.

When Ray leaves the ring, he blisters the speed bag for several rounds (all the while wearing a less than conscious smile – he's very happy), then polishes off the session with a couple of rounds of rope. Next, he goes with Correa to the massage table.

Ray has suffered a fairly bad rope burn in today's training. The back of his now translucent T-shirt is streaked with blood. Pepé pulls it away from Ray's body and cuts it from his back with a pair of surgical scissors. He then pulls a bottle of rubbing alcohol from under the table and pours it directly on to Ray's wound. As the alcohol makes contact, the finest pugilist of the 1980s, who has been knocked down so few times in a career of almost 200 fights and countless sparring sessions, drops to his knees, noisily sucking air, working hard to suppress a scream.

After Correa finishes, Ray trudges upstairs to shower. I wait about five minutes, then follow and take a seat on a yellow sofa. When he's through towelling off, Ray pulls on a one-piece olive military jumpsuit and a pair of black combat boots. 'Davis, I hope you brought some Bruce-stuff,' he says.

I have a tape in the car, I tell him.

'Hey, man, I'll let you in on something I've never told anybody,' he says, taking a seat beside me and bending forward to tie his boots. 'When I was a kid, I used to come back from Bruce movies and go into my mom's backyard. He fired me up so much I took my fist and drove it into the ground until I made a hole three or four inches deep.' He doesn't look embarrassed by his admission.

Unabashedly, I tell him I did things like that too. Then we stand and walk downstairs. As we step into the main gym, I say, 'You had your legs under you today. Pretty soon, you'll be a totally tuned man.'

'You wait and see,' he says. 'In another two weeks I'll be able to catch guys with right hands like this.'

There's a wall a half-step to our left. In one movement, he falls to the plaster, slapping his shoulders against it, rocks on his heels for leverage and, rolling back to his toes, springs a punch a couple inches past the right side of my jaw. As he rips the right, he allows its momentum to carry him behind me, where there's no way I'd be able to counter. I spin and look at him. His eyes are hard-bright.

'Watch this,' he says, snaking his open right hand past my raised left fist, but much more slowly now, across the shoulder and behind my neck, which he lightly clasps.

153

His hand is as small as a woman's. The act is gentle; it seems almost a gesture of friendship. Until he pulls my head down into a crisp left uppercut, which he stops a half-inch from my chin. I'm stunned by the heat I feel coming from him.

'After that, you could try this,' he says, powdering my hips and abdomen with a patented 'Sugar' Ray body combination. I don't see the punches, but feel them as they dust my torso.

'For me, that wouldn't be natural,' I say, forcing myself to speak, pretending not to be in awe.

'What would *you* do?' he asks, moving back a little and watching me closely. He's testing – he intends to find out exactly what I know about his art.

'I think I'd try to angle a hook over here, maybe push him off like this, probably jab behind it to finish the combination or open him up for something else.'

I place my palms high on Ray's chest and shove him back about eighteen inches. He keeps good position and balance.

But in the act of pushing 'Sugar' Ray Leonard, I have now gone with him to a world beyond words, to a universe so intimate, honest and immediate – and so dangerously between two people – that, even with my ring experience, it just about scares the leaves off my tree.

I see the look he wants to hide (he's lowered a reptilian lid inside his eyes) but can't. He's wearing an ever-so-slight smile. This says that something in the way I've pushed him has told him more about my limitations and abilities than he could have learned through many hours of verbal sparring. In the interminable moments of facing off, fighters never want opponents to know what they can or cannot do. In this way, making war is always about lying to the man in front of you. But now, whether or not I like it (and I don't), I am standing naked in front of 'Sugar' Ray Leonard.

'I need to tell you something,' I say, having no clue what words will come from my mouth. 'I used to not like you,' I say. 'And I couldn't admit it was because I was envious. In a way, I wanted to be who you were. I guess now I don't need that any more.'

He gives me a look only slightly less than stunned. Then he studies me dead on; finally, his eyes soften. 'Hey, man, ain't no thing,' he says, clapping a hand on my shoulder. 'How about you come with me to my mom's and chow down on some Chinese food?'

I accept Ray's offer with considerable relief.

Numerous other world champion boxers have been inspired by Lee, including Mike Tyson, who buys hundreds of martial arts movies and, like Leonard, has said he learned explosiveness from watching Lee in *Enter the Dragon*. It's a lesson that hasn't always served Tyson well.

And there's Hector 'Macho' Camacho. 'I got an Elvis room and a Bruce Lee room in my house,' Camacho reveals, 'with posters and pictures everywhere and furniture and stuff.' When club-hopping, Camacho has been known to sport white traditional Chinese garb modelled on what Lee wore in *Fist of Fury*.

And, at the age of fifteen, influenced by Lee, southpaw defensive phantom Wilfredo Benitez became the youngest-ever world champion pugilist. Benitez's nickname was 'The Dragon'. He's the fighter from whom Leonard won his first world title. On that day in the ring, with big lights playing across their gleaming faces, torsos and arms and legs, Leonard and Benitez seemed mirror images of each other.

In addition to inspiring many professional athletes, Lee has influenced the way every single action-movie hero and heroine has moved in fights since the mid-1970s. And he has inspired video-game programmers and stunt guys. 'Almost all stunt co-ordinators who came after Bruce were influenced,' says Tan. 'Any movie or TV show with fights in it – *Raiders of the Lost Ark*, *Star Wars*, *Buffy the Vampire Slayer*, animated fights in *The Lion King* – it doesn't matter what. If you know what you're looking at, you'll catch camera angles and martial arts techniques from Bruce's scenes, stuff Bruce invented. He contributed so much to the industry that has never been recognized.'

But did Lee make a significant contribution to anything more ennobling than the (rather sociopathic) prettification of violence? Indeed he did. Perhaps the best, most life-affirming, of Lee's legacy is this: a popularization of forward-looking art and philosophy.

When asked why he had no rear windows in his automobiles, Frank Lloyd Wright answered, 'I don't look behind me.'

It is a statement I believe Bruce Lee would have admired.

'What we're doing is sort of musical *jeet kune do*,' says acclaimed electric bass reinventor Victor Wooten of Béla Fleck and the Flecktones. The body of Wooten's custom-designed instrument has been emblazoned with a porcelain black-and-white yin and yang symbol. Inspired by Lee, Wooten has studied wing chun and other martial disciplines since his teen years; he often wears Bruce Lee T-shirts on stage. He and his brother, the pyrotechnic percussionist for the Flecktones, Roy 'Futureman' Wooten, both consider Lee to be among their major musical and spiritual mentors. They say they learned much about the complex rhythms they eventually used in their music-making by growing up watching Lee and his movies.

Where Lee integrated fighting forms of the world into his art, the compositions that the multi-Grammy Award-winning Flecktones compose and play are informed by such formerly disparate sources as r&b, classical, jazz, bluegrass, Celtic and Cajun; and Middle Eastern, East Indian, Chinese, Japanese and American folk. 'No way as way,' says Roy 'Futureman' Wooten, winking. As was true of the martial art which Lee developed, Flecktone tunes are at once simple *and* complex, substantive and very accessible. This music is playfully American, yet international – and, to many people, including me, profoundly cosmic. And it is played with a bristling majesty that, like Lee's onscreen performances, can seem beyond the capacity of normal human beings.

Banjoist Béla Fleck explains his art without explaining it away. 'You can't name what we do,' he says, implying something tantamount to the spiritual. 'To us, this is life. We just write and play the music.'

To me, Fleck and the Wootens and their music verify that there's little unique about 'Bruce Lee's' philosophy. Arguably, 'Lee's' organic ideas are the major working theory of art over the past hundred years. And, as is true for artisans from Monet to Wright to Miles Davis to Fleck and novelist Tom Robbins (who studies martial art in Seattle with Lee student Jim DeMile), this non-way of approaching art and life seems as much biological as consciously controlled by people: it arrived in the world as if by osmosis.

Among other 'biological' movements in which Lee had a role: the post-World War Two Western ideal of the superior Christian, Anglo-Saxon, mannerly tough guy (*à la* Duke Wayne and Rocky Marciano), humbled by the Koreans, crippled by Ali and resolutely de-limbed by the Viet Cong, this bad old white-boy was killed dead, and replaced in the public consciousness, by little bitty Bruce Lee.

As millions of tiny twits like me – whether we were yellow, black, white or brown – first saw Lee on big enveloping movie screens, we no longer felt so little, so powerless. Lee even managed to help a few of us swim out of our bowls of sad soup and find something resembling real dry-land lives.

Others, however, became still more enthralled.

In the late 1980s one Bruce Lee fan mailed videocassettes to Linda Lee and several of Lee's former students in which, while throwing a series of round-kicks towards a video camera, he claimed to be the son of Lee and Lindsay *The Bionic Woman* Wagner and then confessed his desire to 'connect with' his 'big brother Brandon' and 'little sister Shannon'. The Lees' family attorney sent notice to this fellow that he was not to approach Linda Lee or her children. He was last heard from in Seattle, where he'd changed his name to Dalton Lee (the name of the Patrick Swayze character in the 1980s action-movie *Roadhouse*), and had moved to a motel near Bruce Lee's grave.

And there was Mikey Miyazaki, the son of a wealthy Tokyo businessman who, in his early twenties, used his father's money to make his bedroom into a composite of several *Enter the Dragon* sets. For more than a decade, televisions were mounted to the ceiling in the room's corners and Miyazaki perpetually played a different Lee movie on all four monitors and wore Lee-style Chinese garb for pyjamas.

Then there's Blade Leong, who lived in LA, claimed he was Bruce Lee (after all, they shared the same initials) and made his wife dress like Linda Lee did in the 1960s, down to her one-piece shifts and beehive hairstyle.

Another true believer was retired Mongolian physician, Ichinorov Dendev, who, in the fall of 1993, in celebration of the twentieth anniversary of Lee's death, set off on a nine-month pilgrimage during which he and two disciples unsuccessfully attempted to walk across the Bering Straits from Mongolia to Seattle to place flowers on the grave of the god of martial art.

More infamously, a young Londoner sent letters to the British martial arts publication, *Kung-fu Monthly* (the magazine's unofficial motto is: 'All Lee, all the time'), in which he tried to explain that the word God was an acronym for the movie, *Game of Death*. He eventually hijacked a bus and rammed it through a shopfront screaming, 'I'm Bruce Lee, I'm God. I'm Bruce Lee, I'm God.'

And there's the Elvis Presley and Bruce Lee acolyte in northern Idaho, who named his son Brandon, his daughters Shannon and Lisa Marie, and who changed his own name to Jesus Lee Presley.

Then, on 20 July 1986, Betty Ting Pei gave birth to a son, who, she told friends, was the reincarnation of Bruce Lee.

And I have also had a role in the proliferation of the Bruce Lee (non)gospel.

In addition to naming my son Isaac *Lee* Miller (after my father, Roy Lee Miller, and Bruce Lee), in 1992 I wrote articles for *Sports Illustrated*, for *Sport* magazine, and for the *Los Angeles Times* about world kick-boxing champion and actress Kathy Long, the female Bruce Lee in muscularity, strength-level and litheness, and yet another kung fu child born in a year of the dragon – 1964.

Fred Weintraub read two of my pieces and asked me to script a ninety-minute film documentary about Lee for Warner Brothers. Weintraub said his feature would be released on videocassette, then cable TV, around the twentieth anniversary of Lee's death and the theatrical premiere of *Dragon*.

I accepted his offer, excited about the possibility of developing the first honest Bruce Lee documentary and doing so for the guy who had co-produced Lee's only American film. *Enter the Dragon*, which was made for less than 600,000 dollars, made Weintraub self-sustainably wealthy. During an early production meeting in his Century City office, despite having courted his newly contracted writer by regularly referring to himself as Lee's 'dear friend', Weintraub said, 'You have to understand, movies aren't art: they're commerce. I don't care about the truth of this putz's life. You don't have to exactly say he was fuckin' Marilyn Monroe – but you better damn well imply it.'

Badly needing the money, and still committed to doing the best work about Lee I had in me, I stayed with Weintraub's project. I researched Lee's life as completely as Weintraub would allow, trying to puzzle out some kind of honest story about the guy, travelling to and from New York, Los Angeles, San Francisco, Seattle and Hong Kong, spending time with, and talking to, Lee's students, friends, co-workers and some of his family. (When Brandon Lee was shot, Weintraub's assistant was on the phone trying to arrange a date and time for me to interview him.)

In addition to writing the script for Weintraub's feature, I worked as researcher, facilitator, interviewer and line producer. The story I developed was apparently more to my liking than Weintraub's. Although I received sole screen credit for Fred's show, hardly a word I wrote was used in the film. Weintraub's co-producer in this project was Tom Kuhn, the former Warner exec for whom Lee had auditioned for the starring role in the *Kung-fu* TV series.

I called my script, *Death by Misadventure: The Mysterious Life of Bruce Lee*, not a great title, admittedly. Weintraub's and Kuhn's show, however, was released under the thoroughly dubious name, *Curse of the Dragon*.

30

1

BRUCE LEE WAS the progenitor of post-modern martial art. The two questions I'm most often asked about him are: How did he die? And how good was he as a martial artist?

Well, as best as I can tell, he was plenty wonderful. Probably the best martial practitioner of his time. Does this make him the best fighter in the world, then or ever? Was he the real live twentieth-century god of martial art?

This is some of what we know: Bruce Lee was blessed with good long arms (Dan Inosanto says, 'Bruce had the reach of a six-footer'), incredible initiation speed and reaction time, and he hit big-hard compared to most others in the Asian fighting disciplines. 'Bruce had phenomenal attributes,' confirms Joe Lewis. 'Amazing speed, power, strength, reflexes.'

Says Hayward Nishioka, 'He was the quickest person I've ever seen. In that area he was king. And he knew it. He had that same cockiness Americans have. Americans say, "I'm arrogant, and I'll show you why. I can do it. I'm good." '

World-class athlete Kareem Abdul Jabbar was more than a little impressed with Lee's prowess. 'He had cunning, killer instinct and the will to dominate. And incredible athletic skills: balance, eye–hand co-ordination, timing. And all that driven by a very intense will.'

Yet, as a fighter, Lee had serious anatomical inadequacies, including a pointed chin, a narrow jaw and long thin neck; small bones, particularly his wrists and ankles; and horrible vision – he was terribly nearsighted – he couldn't see ten feet from his face without corrective lenses. It goes without saying that it's tough to get out of the way of fists and feet if you can't tell they're being beamed at you. And, considering the circumstances of his death, as well as his physical stature, it seems reasonable to say that he may have been a markedly fragile human being.

Dissecting Lee's film battles also reveals that, although there's little doubt he understood the necessity of co-ordinated offensive and defensive movement, preached it and wanted to move beautifully, compared to boxers he was not a consummate mover: he was pretty good at in and out, forward and backward movements – he pranced instead of gliding, though, which sacrifices power while magnifying the effects of blows with which your opponent(s) catch(es) you. And he had little idea how effectively to accomplish more subtle side-to-side movements. Also, he often held his head high and stiff instead of keeping it low, serpentine and mobile. As has been shown when martial-arts trained fighters attempt to box professionally, their lack of lateral mobility and a general upper body stiffness often helps to sit them down hard on the seat of their jammies.

And, as is true of most guys in the martial disciplines, Lee was not street-rough. He was middle-class tough, at most. Not that there's anything wrong with this. Indeed, in lots of ways, it's comforting to discover that Lee wasn't a hard-core tough guy. Like most of us, he was a person hoping and trying to cope, moment to moment, with the life that was presented to him.

Yet, if the way he treated his kind, timid wife and many of his students is an indication, some of his coping behaviour was less than admirable.

'It was my birthday. And we're down at the studio,' says Lee's friend and assistant instructor, Dan Inosanto. 'Bruce said, "Dan, let's spar a little." Then he turned that light switch of his on and suddenly it was a different person. He hit me one in the solar plex, one in the cheek. And I went down. I'm dazed, shaking my head – and he's laughing. He says, "Bring out the birthday cake." And he's singing happy birthday and laughing. Bruce says, "I just had to knock you out for your twenty-fourth birthday, Dan." '

Lewis claims there were numerous times when he tried to get Lee to spar with him. 'Bruce didn't spar anybody, except a couple of those guys who ran around sucking up to him. But there was one time he set me up. We're training and a couple of his students are standing around. He says, "Joe, fire that forehand strike you're working on." I fired it, he slipped it, and he said, "Come on, Joe, do it again." I did. And he says, "Just once more, Joe." The third time I fired the punch, he slipped it and came back with that triple punch you see right at the beginning of *Enter the Dragon*. He goes, *Ba-ba-bam*, fires the three shots, hits me square between the eyes. He suckered me. And it took him three tries to pull it off. Next thing I hear, his students are running around saying Bruce kicked my ass, completely showed me up. I'll tell you right now – I never, ever, sparred with Bruce. It was never that open with Bruce, not once. Never the possibility of give and take, moment to moment, let's really get down and do it. Almost anybody, and I mean anybody, can make you look stupid setting you up like Bruce did me.'

How do these stories relate to who Lee would have been as a fighter? They provide evidence that he was a bit of a bully. And what we're exploring when we evaluate Lee, as much as mechanics, is metaphysics. Bullies are often limited fighters who can be shocked out of their best stuff when they encounter wilful opponents. 'To whip a bully, you need to consistently break his spirit or have a stronger spirit,' Leonard says. 'The important thing to beat any fighter is to whip him mentally and emotionally, to knock down his spirit and make him believe he can be stopped.'

This is a lesson I had to learn first-hand. On several occasions, when I was vying to become four-limbed lightning, I was shown (usually kindly, sometimes gently; once or twice with some malice) that I could be beaten into the ground by wilful, experienced guys who didn't have half my speed, a third of my brights, a fourth of my conditioning, a fifth of my skill. Not to mention what happened whenever I climbed through the ropes with an obvious superior.

Stepping into the dank, musty gym, the Champ winks at spectators and approaches the ring with a big easy smile, taking measured, self-contained steps on the balls of the feet, shoulders slightly back, chest out, head level. There's a regality to it. It is watchful, a little removed; cool but not snooty. As if the skin is listening. As if every pore contains a satellite dish. Boxers call this the champions' walk. Both Ali and Leonard move this way.

Using yellow elastic bandaging, the Champ quickly and expertly wraps wrists and hands, and ritualistically tugs on a pair of shining fire-engine-red twelve-ounce gloves. After wrapping ankles and feet, the Champ steps barefoot through the ropes to meet a strutting sparring partner. The sparring partner outweighs the titleholder by a good twenty pounds.

The bell rings and the Champ dances a few steps to the left, measuring the opponent with a couple jabs that miss. Now inside, the Champ digs a straight right in under the sparring partner's ribcage, springs a hook in near the right kidney, crisply doubles it to the head, then dances to the side and out of reach, her blondish hair bounding behind her, cascading down her shoulders and spilling across her back in ringlets. She's wearing matching black shorts and loose-fitting tank-top.

She bends to the right and snaps a jab into my nose. My ears are already ringing from the good hook she caught me with. Now I blink back tears and stare at her. She's startlingly good-looking – high cheekbones and clear bright expansive eyes the hue of Western skies. Deltoids are large, firm, round; forearm muscle groups dance. Her musculature is so defined that fat cells seem to have no place to hide in her body. There's an aura of healthy tomboy androgyny around her: she's Doris Day in Ellen Barkin's body. All of this, of *her*, is more than a bit disarming.

Five-time women's featherweight world kick-boxing champ Kathy Long drops her gloves to her sides, sticks her neck and face forward, teasing me. She pulls her head back and away when I try to pump a quick jab into her chin and immediately leans back in, rapping my nose with a shocking straight left. It's a slick 'Sugar' Ray Leonard trick I can't believe I've fallen for. My eyes haven't quit watering from the last shot she caught me with; there's no way I'll stop them now. My mouth feels fat and swollen, as if I'm sitting in a dentist's chair getting all my molars drilled into at once; it tastes like I've been trying to suck out the insides of someone's hundred-year-old bathroom plumbing.

Long slings a Thai-style switch-kick towards my head, which I slip. Before she gets her foot back to the floor, I manage to stick her (*Finally!*) with a long firm left; she makes me pay by kicking me hard on the inside of my left thigh. The slapping sound is explosive in the small room. I feel the pain after I hear the sound; a thousand fire ants sink scalpel-sharp nippers into some of the most tender flesh on my body.

No matter what, though, I'm not going to show Kathy

she's got to me. I dance to the left, trying to seem relaxed and casual. She comes on, her lips squeezed together tightly, looking tombstone serious. I move to the ropes then lean my upper body to the left, as if I'll disengage. She goes for my draw; I thump her with a straight right lead that snaps her head back sixty degrees. She's stunned – maybe. I move in fast and hard with both hands, shooting the best stuff I've got.

She covers up. The hooks and uppercuts I zip towards her head catch nothing but gloves and sweat. I step back and spring a left side-kick towards her belly. She grits her teeth, deflects the kick outwardly with her left elbow, turning me towards her, opening me up. She roars from her shell, drilling me hard and deep to my right shin with her own shin. The noise I hear is unmistakably that of bone against bone. The sound makes me wince. To put some space between Kathy and me, I slide off to the right. I'm OK, my leg is fine, just a little numb, I don't feel a thing. Then, without another shot being thrown, my leg gives out and I unexpectedly find myself looking up at her from the canvas. A goddamned delayed reaction. I feel like a soiled shirt tossed to the floor.

That's when the *real* pain arrives, powerful enough to separate thoughts from words. Everything I look at throbs. The air around me goes red-tinged. My leg feels as if it had decided to remove itself from my body and run into a wrought-iron coffee table at fifty miles an hour.

Although I can't hear a thing because of the white noise going off in my skull, I know I'm groaning loud and making ugly faces and looking about as dumb as a person can look. I roll to my right, hugging my shin, rocking from side to side; a father, clutching his young son's right hand, squinches up his face and subconsciously bends to the right to rub his own shin. Embarrassed, I roll in the other direction and close my eyes.

Kathy comes over, kneels and tugs me to my feet. She places an arm around my waist to support me. I hobble from the ring, eyes pointed towards the floor. I can't carry weight on my right leg. Kathy gets me to a corner and sits me on a stool. As Kathy walks away, a smirking, curly red-haired trainer comes over and straps ice packs to both my thighs and my calves. 'You just got beat up by a skirt,' she says, trying not to giggle in my face.

'Hey, that's my life story,' I say.

I limp across the room and take a seat beside Kathy as she autographs publicity photos for a clot of spectators – 'Hugs and punches from Kathy Long, five-time world champ.'

After everyone but Kathy and I has left, she reaches into a pocket of her shorts and produces a necklace with an attached small gold boxing glove. It's the symbol amateur boxers wear who have won Golden Gloves tournaments. The difference is that Kathy's pendant has a one-fourth carat diamond that's been set in the palm of the glove. She straps this talisman about her neck and smiles a smile that levels me even more than her fists and feet. She smiles again, waves for me to follow her, and she walks the champions' walk back out on to the street.

No doubt about it: Bruce Lee would have turned *my* scrawny little skin inside out and hung it on a coat rail. And surely he could have done the same with many famous movie-martial-monkeys who arrived after his death. Yet Bruce Lee was untested as a fighter – and it isn't pointless to note that he seemed to prefer it that way. Who knows if he had the will to transcend his competition in those most feverish of battles, where wilful fighters take your most stupendous shots and keep coming at you – or sometimes simply smile at you. Everyone can be beaten – not just little writer-guys who've been known to wear Bruce Lee T-shirts. And even Lee himself didn't know whether he had the stuff it takes to keep going to the well; to believe, after he brought up an empty bucket or two, that he needed to keep going back.

2

Coburn: 'That still pond he was talking about. That still pond in the middle of action, that pond deep inside. I don't think he ever found that.'

3

Jabbar: 'Bruce wished he had more friends, but he didn't want to be that vulnerable. He had to keep up a kind of mystique.'

4

Coburn: 'Wherever we were, he was always the centre of attention. He was always demonstrating his ability to control people. And wherever he wasn't in control, he left.'

5

'What's your style?' Bruce Lee is asked by an antagonist in *Enter the Dragon*.

'You can call it "the art of fighting without fighting",' Lee replies.

6

Bruce Lee was possibly the first martial practitioner to have trained *as* a 'scientific' fighter. Psychologically, he *needed* to be regarded – by himself and others – as a fighter. These factors speak to Lee's motivation and commitment as a martial artist. But was he a *real* fighter?

'Angelo Dundee never fought,' says Lewis, 'but he understands the science of fighting. Robert De Niro looks great as Jake La Motta in *Raging Bull*. When he's standing in front of a mirror, he throws some good-looking punches. I must've heard Bruce say a hundred times, "You can't swim without getting in the water, Joe." But, what Bruce did is he *thought* about sparring. Always analysing, always figuring something out. Partly to make himself look good because he understood fighting, partly to look good in movies. All the time standing on the shore watching other guys swim.

'People who do something over and over do it because they like it. Why do they like it? Because it empowers them, makes them feel special. Since Bruce wasn't fighting anybody who was good, why was it empowering to analyse all that karate and wrestling and boxing? If you're not gonna get in the ring and look good, then you want to *feel* good. And what's gonna make you feel good is when you know something – and people *believe* you know something. You want to understand Bruce Lee, what makes the boy tick. It's pretty simple – it's vanity, baby.'

7

'Substitute the word "swimmer" for "fighter",' says Lewis. 'This was the greatest *swimmer* of all time. He woulda beat everybody else, ever.'

'Was he?' I ask. 'How many times did he win the Olympics?'

' "Aw, man, he didn't have to do all that." That's what those JKD guys claim. "He was *beyond* all that," they say.

'Now here, this guy's never competed, never been to a

swim meet, we've never seen him really swim. We don't even know how many swimming lessons he had, really. Do you see what I mean?

'Put another word in place of "fighter", does all of it start to sound stupid or what?'

8

How would little man's messiah Bruce Lee have done against *big*, experienced tough guys of his time: Ali, Lewis (who was recently voted 'Fighter of the Century' by fellow martial arts competitors, and who in 1976 in their one – albeit playful – encounter, *immediately* had Ali tied up and powerless on the floor), Frazier, George Foreman, footballer Jim Brown, undefeated collegiate wrestler Dan Gable, show-wrestler Gorgeous George?

'Let's put it this way,' says Lewis, 'if "Sugar" Ray Robinson got in a ring with Ali, his mainspring woulda got broke before his clock ever got wound. Thunder that big guys throw, you can't believe how hard they hit. When they hit a little guy like Bruce, it could literally kill him.'

9

Then there's one more, less celebrated bloke, among Lee's contemporaries, whose connection with Lee is worth noting.

'Without question, he's the toughest man alive,' says Chuck Norris. 'And I'm not the only fella who feels that way.'

Norris is referring not to his co-star in *Way of the Dragon*, but to seventy-year-old 'Judo' Gene LeBell. For almost fifty years, LeBell has been a world-class *judoka* (as a 165-pound competitor, he won the overall national AAU championships in both 1954 and 1955; yes, he chumped the heavyweights), a world heavyweight wrestling champion, one of the most respected stuntfolks in television and movies (he launched his career as George Reeves's stunt double on the 1950s *Superman* TV series and in the late 1990s is still in demand) and a karate instructor.

LeBell began his education in personal combat as an aspiring pugilist. 'My mother, Aileen Eaton, owned the Olympic Auditorium in Los Angeles,' he says. 'I grew up sparring guys like Ray Robinson and Archie Moore. I wanted to be a professional boxer, but my mother wouldn't let me. She said it was too rough, I'd get hurt. So that's when I began hangin' out with 'rasslers.'

As he's speaking, LeBell is leaning back on a swivel chair behind the little maple desk in his Santa Monica Mountains work-out cabin. He's barefoot; his long flat feet are stretched out in front of him and they're crossed atop his desk. He's a medium-big man with a lopsided tough-guy smile and a shock of thin red hair that he combs straight back but which never seems to stay. His is not an untested face. LeBell's flattened countenance is reminiscent of an aesthetic most often encountered when watching Broderick Crawford movies. This afternoon, he's wearing his idea of traditional training garb: a dramatically faded, torn and threadbare black belt (the same strap of material he's worn since the 1960s) and a mid-calf-length, pale *pink* gi.

'Mom knew 'rasslers were swave and gentil,' LeBell says, puffing himself up with feigned haughtiness. 'She knew they wouldn't hurt little ole me.'

LeBell places his feet on the floor and stands. 'From them, I learned to like to *stir-rettcchhh* people.' He abruptly leans forward across his desk with eyes full-moon wide and mouth open in a ''rassler's' growl; he moves his hands in front of his chest like he's milking a full-grown rhinoceros.

171

LeBell has 'stir-rettcchhhed' lots of tough guys over the years, including Milo Savage in 1963, in the first ring contest to have featured a martial artist against a boxer. He's also stretched many of the world's best martial practitioners, including Norris, Lewis and Stone.

'And about anybody else he's wanted to,' Norris says.

'I was a stuntman on *The Green Hornet*,' says LeBell. 'Bruce was a hard guy to get to know, always actin' kinda sophisticated. So, when I got tired of it, I'd pick him up, sling him over my shoulder and run all around the set with him. He'd scream, "Put me down, put me down." I reckon I teased him so much I eventually got him to loosen up a little. He got to where he took jokes pretty good – specially if ya'd grabbed him round the neck.'

Says Lewis of LeBell's encounters with the god of gung fu: 'When Gene squeezed him, Bruce'd make this high-pitched squeaking noise.'

WHEN LEE'S LIFE is seriously studied it becomes clear, almost immediately, that he was not who we have thought he was. He was neither a Ronald Wong-Donald at work in some chop-socky restaurant where feature flicks can be served up for corporate lunch money, nor was he an all-wise, mystically empowered ascetic.

Perhaps the highest compliment Lee's own fans could pay him – and themselves – would be to look past the screen caricature, beyond the high-kicking clichés, to recognize some of the ways he resembles the rest of us. One of the most important things Lee has helped me see is this: any and all notions we have carried with us about him, and who he was, are, at best, reductionist. And what's true for Lee applies to the rest of us: 'I am human, and nothing human is foreign to me.'

Unlike Lee's swaggering, 'I am all styles . . .' fantasy, Terence's statement is not positivist, is not about work, about muscle strain; it's a declaration of his, and our, basic humanity. In nature there's no such thing as paradox. There's only that which seems paradoxical. Though we may be uncomfortable with it, in many ways we're all Mother Teresa *and* Jeffrey Dahmer, Gandhi and Hitler, Claude Debussy and Mick Jagger. And everyone else human beings have been and can be.

When considering Lee, other American tales are remembered: Scott and Zelda, Marilyn, the Kennedys, James Dean: dreamers, and purveyors, of the dream, who, like Icarus, found themselves a bit too close to the sun.

Jesus, Alexander the Great, Joan of Arc and, yes, Bruce Lee died young enough to believe that there was something about themselves they *had* to develop, and about the world that *had* to be changed. As we mature, some of us come to another understanding. We hope to recognize things as they are and to accept them.

Yet, as a species, we ache for saviours. And this is understandable: it's a damned hard world. There's so much each of us wishes we could be liberated from every moment of our lives: mortality, morbidity, pain, unrequited dreams. Among the most common saviours our species has developed are work, athletics, family, lovers, social clubs, institutions, philosophies, science, political leaders, storytelling, religions, idols, art, ourselves.

Should human beings survive for a couple of hundred more years, I believe that our fame-driven century will have spawned several arrogant American gods: Muhammad Ali, Elvis Presley and Bruce Lee.

Once *the* Spokesperson for self-actualization, Ali has lived plenty (and been beaten up enough) to recognize the myopia of that youthful, basically American religion. Ali's own weighty yet gentle myth has become this: No one, not even The Greatest of All Times, can defy gravity.

'The man who talks about the Tao, does not know the Tao,' wrote Chuang Tzu.

'Things people praise me for, I didn't do those myself,' I've heard the older Ali say. 'We don't choose to draw air into our own lungs. We don't decide where we're born or who we are.'

Says Lewis, 'When I first met Bruce, he told me, "Joe, I'm not a master. I'm a student. I'm learning, evolving. I don't call myself a master. I'm a student master."

'I like that,' Lewis says, laughing, ' "a student master".

And I'm sorry Bruce seemed to lose that sense of proportion.'

'There was nothing wrong with Bruce that a few years wouldn't have fixed,' Siliphant says. 'If he'd lived, I think he would've become a genuinely great man.'

Perhaps the most resonant Bruce Lee myth is that he was murdered by his own ambition, by his arrogance in believing he could create himself.

I use no way as way, have no limitation as limitation.

A more poignant epitaph for our century would be difficult to find.

YET, FINALLY. THIS is what matters most to me about Bruce Lee.

At dusk on a September evening in 1973 I stepped blinking into a nickel-and-dime cinema in a village in the mountains of North Carolina. And in that large, dark, warm room where dreams prowl, there was a shock in seeing him.

For the next ninety-three minutes, everything was as blinding, noisy and insanely beautiful as digitally enhanced film of a nuclear weapons blast.

At the end of *Enter the Dragon*, when I walked from the Banner Elk Bijou, everything seemed different – brilliant, interesting, vivid as a just-sliced orange on a winter window sill. And it stayed that way.

Sitting here now, all these years later, staring yet again at a couple of autographed photos of Lee, with all I've learned about him, his death and his life, I still see heat and light around him. And I feel startled by his presence.

Almost thirty years after being tugged from his shell, Foetus remains grateful to Bruce Lee. Through Lee and Ali, I came to train, not only to become an athlete, but a person. I became open to the possibilities and to the mysteries, to the rhythms of life. People climb mountains not because they are there, but to feel a sense of greater connection. Through Lee, I climbed a few mountains and then knew I was connected. And today, at the age of forty-seven, I don't believe anyone can ask more than that of his mentors.